LEADING

LIBRARIES

LEADING

LIBRARIES

HOW TO CREATE A SERVICE CULTURE

Wyoma vanDuinkerken and Wendi Arant Kaspar

ala
editions

AN IMPRINT OF THE AMERICAN LIBRARY ASSOCIATION
CHICAGO 2015

Wyoma vanDuinkerken received an MLIS in 2000 from the University of Illinois-Urbana Champaign and an MA in Islamic studies in 1997 from McGill University, Canada. She joined Texas A&M University in 2004 and received tenure in 2010. She is currently the director of the Joint Library Facility but has held a number of additional roles at Texas A&M University Libraries, including coordinator of Cataloging Record Support, coordinator of Acquisitions Monographs, reference librarian and administrator of Virtual Reference. Her research interests include virtual reference, project management, acquisitions, organizational change management, servant leadership, and library administration. She has written numerous articles and book chapters, and she just completed her first monograph, *The Challenge of Library Management: Leading with Emotional Engagement.* She served as coeditor-in-chief for the *Journal of Academic Librarianship.*

Wendi Arant Kaspar received an MLS from the University of Washington in 1994 and an MS in Human Resources Management from Texas A&M University–College Station. She joined Texas A&M University in 1996, received tenure in 2002, and was promoted to professor in 2011. Her research interests include human resources and management in libraries, innovation in library services and outreach. She has written numerous articles and book chapters and has served as coeditor of *Library Administration and Management* and coeditor-in-chief of *The Journal of Academic Librarianship.*

© 2015 by the American Library Association

Extensive effort has gone into ensuring the reliability of the information in this book; however, the publisher makes no warranty, express or implied, with respect to the material contained herein.

ISBNs
978-0-8389-1312-3 (paper)
978-0-8389-1316-1 (PDF)
978-0-8389-1317-8 (ePub)
978-0-8389-1318-5 (Kindle)

Library of Congress Cataloging-in-Publication Data
VanDuinkerken, Wyoma.
  Leading libraries : how to create a service culture / Wyoma vanDuinkerken and Wendi Arant Kaspar.
    pages cm
  Includes bibliographical references and index.
  ISBN 978-0-8389-1312-3 (print : alk. paper) 1. Public services (Libraries) 2. Library personnel management. 3. Leadership. 4. Customer relations. I. Arant Kaspar, Wendi, 1971– II. Title.
  Z711.V36 2015
  025.5—dc23
                            2014045790

Cover design by Alejandra Diaz.
Text design and composition in the Adobe Garamond typeface by Adrianna Sutton.

♾ This paper meets the requirements of ANSI/NISO Z39.48–1992 (Permanence of Paper).

Printed in the United States of America
19 18 17 16 15   5 4 3 2 1

CONTENTS

....

PREFACE

....

While writing this book, we struggled with a very fundamental concept: leadership. It has given us pause at every turn. Perhaps it is because nomenclature and detail have always been important to our profession. We know this to be true because when we first started discussing the concept of this book with the American Library Association (ALA), the working title was actually *Managing People in Libraries: Creating and Sustaining Servant Leadership in Service Organizations*, a title that spoke very much to the model and the values that we wanted to convey. However, while ALA was interested in the concept and thought that it would have appeal, there were questions about the use of the word *servant*—not concerns that we were using servant leadership as a lens to look at management in our profession, but rather the apprehension that the use of the word "servant" would be distasteful to the audience, particularly those readers who would be interested in reading a book about leadership.

Perhaps the term *leadership* has confounded us because it seems always to be contingent upon a position of authority or, in other words, management titles, and what is discussed in this book makes no such assumption. Certainly, those in positions of authority have more opportunities to lead and certainly more responsibility. As Voltaire is reputed to have said, "With great power comes great responsibility." Strangely, a leader, particularly a leader who places service above all, is practically the antithesis of the traditional authoritarian model in libraries. More than that, there is a pervasive argument about whether a true leader seeks power (or authority or control) or has a more altruistic purpose. Many leadership theories have taken one side or the other of this argument, explicitly or by assumption. That said, if service is at the core of librarianship (and there may be arguments against that as the profession evolves), then it should also be at the core of leadership in libraries.

We have searched through leadership books and management articles, philosophical treatises and political documents, even dictionaries and thesauri, searching for a word that would convey the essence of leadership without the presumption of some sort of hierarchy. *Entrepreneur* was an attractive term, particularly in view of its recent popularity in library literature. Advocate, champion, activist, frontier, guide, advisor, visionary, pioneer, revolutionary, and many more words were all considered and rejected because of the political connotations that many of these terms have assumed.

So, we will stick to the term *leadership*. That said, we want it understood that we are not talking about the standard definition of leadership.

The title of this book was chosen very deliberately. We wanted to explore leading in libraries—not leadership in terms of being a leader (largely assumed by position authority) but the act of leading—with a focus on what it means to lead, the acts and behaviors that manifest and how they are derived from individual interactions with others and how they impact a larger organization.

This book is not precisely a how-to, although it will provide some examples and cases along with some reflective exercises and tools so that those who are so inclined can see how a commitment to service manifests in action. The service orientation is fundamental. Many management books and indeed many managers prescribe certain behaviors that are leadership behaviors or management best practices, but there is no commitment, no sincerity behind those actions. What we are discussing goes beyond leading with intention; it is leading with meaning.

Included in this volume are tools for exercising service leadership skills and modeling service leadership behavior. A service commitment is mandatory; otherwise, the efforts lack sincerity and are just going through the motions. As Robert Greenleaf said, "technique without the attitude is phoney."[1]

NOTE

1. Robert K. Greenleaf, *The Servant Leader Within: A Transformative Path* (Mahwah, NJ: Robert K. Greenleaf Center, 2003), 46.

ACKNOWLEDGMENTS

We would like to thank our husbands and children for their patience and support as we researched and wrote this book. We also want to thank our colleagues for inspiring us to write about the importance of service leadership in libraries.

All characters appearing in this work are fictitious. Any resemblance to real persons, living or dead, is purely coincidental.

INTRODUCTION

....

LEADING LIBRARIES: SERVICE
LEADERSHIP IN A SERVICE ORGANIZATION

Introducing and extending a service leadership model into an organization's cultural values and practices can be challenging. Not only does an individual have to be committed to service, but she must be able to communicate that value and the attendant vision to the stakeholders and then follow through with this vision, leading by example. However, for an individual to be a true service leader, she needs to embody the values of service leadership.

Libraries typify a service organization. They are models of public service in that their mission is to serve their patrons, be they faculty and students at a university or at an elementary or high school, citizens of a municipality, officials and employers of a government entity, or stakeholders in a private enterprise. Although libraries are attentive to their clientele, they have struggled to adopt this service value in their internal operations and may not model it for their colleagues and staff.

The foundation of the service leadership model in this book rests on five concepts: conscientiousness, rapport building, encouragement and accountability, innovation, and sustainability. These concepts are formalized or developed through two approaches that embed these values into the policies and processes of the organization: strategy formalizes innovation and strategic thinking and modeling reinforces all five values in the management processes and systems. The importance of these elements of service leadership will be highlighted briefly below, and each will be covered in more depth in a chapter dedicated to that concept.

Conscientiousness

Conscientiousness requires that service is a fundamental motivator. It could also be called character, integrity, or self-awareness. To be conscientious is to encourage an individual to be attentive to who they are and what they believe in. This self-awareness reveals their beliefs and disbeliefs, making them aware of their true values. Service leadership is typified by ethical people who strive to be trustworthy, credible, and committed to their values.

Being conscientious harkens back to Burns' transformational leadership theory and the underlying belief in moral leadership. However, moral leadership relies on the relationship between the leader and the followers, assuming that leaders are conscientious by taking responsibility for their actions while considering the "the fundamental wants and needs, aspirations, and values of the followers."[1] A transforming leadership "ultimately becomes *moral* in that it raises the level of human conduct and ethical aspiration of both leader and led, and thus it has a transforming effect on both."[2] However, service leadership reaches beyond the individual leader with positional authority and is based on the belief that all individuals can be service leaders if they are conscientious.

Chapter 3 will examine the following:

- contemplation and self-reflection;
- awareness;
- consideration and inspiration;
- honesty and integrity;
- authenticity and trust;
- values and decision-making;
- ethical leadership: altruism and service; and
- professional ethics.

Building Rapport

The way in which service leaders build rapport with their colleagues, employees, and customers or patrons is through communication—not just verbal communication but listening as well. As discussed in chapter four, listening is a key aspect of communication and is widely recognized as crucial to any organization. Despite this recognition, most literature examining the development of leaders focuses on the transmitting aspect of communication, such as talking or presenting, in which the leader speaks and the employee listens, which is crucial for the development of leaders. However, this assumes that communication is unidirectional and that the person with positional authority should be delivering the message. Service leaders, on the other hand, understand that two-way communication is fundamental to being a successful leader because it builds rapport with employees and patron, more effectively meeting their needs through the acknowledgment that people are valued and respected for their knowledge, beliefs, and concerns.[3]

But listening also goes beyond what is said, reaches even to what a person is not saying, in a couple of ways. First, a service leader can practice listening by observing an employee or patron's body language, including their eye and facial expressions, and voice fluctuations. This is often considered by some as listening for feelings. Second, a service leader can consider what is missing from the communication: Are there topics that are avoided or things that are specifically not said—the elephant in the room? Such topics are usually significant, if difficult, and very indicative about the climate in an organization. Communication is the foundation of rapport, building a shared understanding and personal investment.

In addition to elaborating on rapport, chapter 4 will examine the intricacies around communicating effectively and building a service leadership organization, including listening to others, encouraging open conversation and moral dialogue, and communicating concern.

Balancing Encouragement and Accountability

The third element of service leadership is to be encouraging to employees and colleagues while holding them and oneself accountable. Encouragement and accountability are really two sides of the same coin. One of the easiest ways for service leaders to encourage their employees is by delegating authority and empowering them to take charge and be leaders themselves. This demonstrates both encouragement and the opportunity for accountability. Leban and Stone believe that if a leader ties these motivators to the overall goals of the organization, then the leader will lay the foundation for a network of support throughout the organization.[4]

Procedural and social justice issues are another way in which service leaders can motivate and encourage their employees to succeed within the organization, holding their management team and themselves accountable. Creating a working environment that is harassment-free, bullying-free, and safe will create a positive work environment where morale is high and retention is high. Although there are federal and state laws as well as organizational rules calling for employers to have this kind of working environment, not all rules and laws are followed. Employees who believe that the leaders of their institution are lacking in procedural and social justice endure an environment of discontent and overall job dissatisfaction.

Chapter 5 will also address the following areas in depth and their implications for service leadership: influence, personal accountability as a library leader, emotional intelligence, empowerment, and social and procedural justice.

Innovation and Evolving Service

Libraries are facing change at an alarming rate; instead of slowing down it is increasing, driven by technology, economics, competing priorities and more. Libraries can approach change in one of two ways: They can drive the change or they can let it drive them. In many instances, the response is more reactive than proactive. Employees are often told how to fix a problem instead of being encouraged to address possible issues before they become problems. Employees understand that the organization that they work for has a culture that punishes instead of praises individual initiative. In an environment in which employees lack the motivation to be innovative, change management becomes impossible because the employees will continue to look up the organizational ladder for permission to change or seek a position in a different organization that will recognize their potential contribution. In the literature as early as the 1880s, James recognized that leaders need help and that their talents didn't always fit with the situation.[5] Davis and Luthans, behavioral theorists, furthered this belief by supporting the idea that a "leader's behavior serves as a discriminative stimulus . . . or cue . . . to evoke the subordinate's task behavior."[6]

Leaders today need their employees to be proactive and show initiative, collaborate smoothly with others, take responsibility for their own professional development, and to be committed to high quality performance standards. Thus employees are needed who feel energetic and dedicated, and who are absorbed by their work. In other words, organizations need engaged workers.[7] In the context of libraries and the change that they constantly face, chapter 6 will also explore:

- creativity, vision, and innovation;
- change management and strategic thinking; and
- challenging the process and risk taking.

Incorporating innovation into the culture can be done by encouraging strategic thinking throughout the organization and applying an inclusive and ongoing strategic-planning process.

STRATEGIC PLANNING: THE PRACTICE OF INNOVATION AND STRATEGIC THINKING

Building on innovation and strategic thinking, strategic planning is the practice or normalization of those values. It is also one of those activities that is generally organization-wide, although it can be done on a micro level within an organization. As stated above, it has traditionally been the managers' responsibility, in conjunction with their employees, to develop a strategic plan for their organization. However, creating a strategic plan is not enough; the organization needs not only to communicate this plan but also to follow through with it. The reason for this is that everyone throughout the organization knows what its values and mission are and also how the day-to-day business should be done.[8]

Following through on values is also critical for a leader. Leaders can do this by modeling the behavior that they value. If, for example, the leader says that he believes his employees should take risks but he is cautious and does not take risks, his behavior will speak volumes to the employee. As a result, employees will not take risks because they do not feel that the leader truly believes in risk taking.

A service leader, on the other hand, motivates employees to get involved in their organization, stressing the importance of strategic planning and how crucial their input is to the organization's future success. Employees, after all, are the life-blood of any organization, and without them the organization would not exist. Without their expert knowledge and their day-to-day understanding of how the work actually gets done, the organization not only would stand still but fall apart. A service leader recognizes that the future of the library rests on the employees' talents and that by engaging them in the planning, they will become more invested in the outcome.

Chapter 7 will address the practices involved in strategic planning and following through, including the following:

- attributes of strategic plan;
- designing the strategic plan;
- crisis management;
- strengths, weaknesses, opportunities, threats;
- developing strategies; and
- assessing the library strategic plan.

SUSTAINING SERVICE AS A VALUE

Creating a service leadership organizational model is not a one-time endeavor; it must be nourished and developed so that it can continue to grow and become engrained in every corner of the organization. In order to sustain the service leadership model, leaders need to recognize that each employee is unique and holds fundamental beliefs and values that affect how they do their jobs. After recognizing these differences, leaders should acknowledge that employees need to be able to grow through professional development activities so that they can develop their strengths and work on their weaknesses. It is important for leaders throughout the organization to encourage professional development, not only for their employees' career development but also for succession planning and innovation for the organization. Ultimately, what the organization needs to create is a learning environment where people are mentored so that they can advance not only in the organization but in their careers.

To encourage a climate of learning, each individual working for the institution must become a steward, committed to everyone who works there. For Bradford and Cohen, the leader needs to be more than just a hero; he needs to be someone who develops his employees in order to build a successful team.[9]

Chapter 8 will discuss how to create a culture of purpose and service that is sustainable and effective, including the following:

- defining the purpose and vision;
- advocating service leadership;
- building an environment of trust;
- performance;
- development and mentoring;
- assessment and feedback;
- systematizing innovation and change; and
- building community, stewardship, and sustaining.

FORMALIZING SERVICE LEADERSHIP IN LIBRARIES: EMBEDDING PROCESSES AND POLICIES

While chapter 8 discusses building a service organization, chapter 9 is concerned with the codification of those values, the policies and procedures that provide the framework. These aspects may be overlooked, considered as less important, but formally documenting procedures and systems in a way that is aligned with values send a clear message. For example, articulating individual or programmatic goals consistent with values and evaluating and rewarding them accordingly will reinforce those values.

Modeling or sustaining the values in the organization is generally also an organization-wide effort requiring buy-in from a high level. However, like strategic planning, it can be done effectively at the unit, project, or service level. Sustaining the culture of service leadership requires more than just espousing its values and pointing to a philosophy document; it necessitates embedding the values within the activities and systems of the organization. In other words, the policies and procedures should reinforce the efforts that the organization wishes to model—in this case, that service in whatever form it takes is superlative. For example, it is a truism that people do what they are rewarded for, and in a service organization, the rewards are likely to be intangible though no less important in signally what is valued and reinforcing desirable behavior. Efforts around merit pay and raises, must go through the hierarchy. However, rewards of a more intrinsic nature can be identified and conferred at any level in the organization.

Chapter 9 will examine how to systematize and model service values in an organization, including the following:

- recruitment and selection;
- learning and personnel development;
- performance evaluation;

- rewards and compensation;
- accountability and termination; and
- leadership development and succession planning.

SERVICE LEADERSHIP IN LIBRARIES

Chapter 10 will focus on service leadership as an organizational value, how that manifests in its mission and activities and how it is perceived by patrons, both internal and external, including the following:

- employee as the patron;
- patron perception of the service culture;
- service quality; and
- organizational culture.

It will also discuss the environment of change in libraries and the necessity of being responsive and staying relevant. The mission of libraries is centered on their mission and providing what their patrons need: the ability to provide effective service is critical.

NOTES

1. James MacGregor Burns, *Leadership* (New York, NY: Harper & Row, 1978), 4.
2. Ibid., 20.
3. Fons Trompenaars and Ed Voerman, *Servant-Leadership Across Cultures* (New York, NY: McGraw Hill, 2010); Robert K. Greenleaf, *Servant Leadership: A Journey into the Nature of Legitimate Power & Greatness* (Mahwah, NJ: Paulist, 1977); James M. Kouzes and Barry Z. Posner, *The Leadership Challenge*, 3rd ed. (San Francisco, CA: Jossey-Bass, 2002).
4. Bill Leban and Romuald Stone, *Managing Organizational Change*, 2nd ed. (Hoboken, NJ: John Wiley, 2008), 136.
5. William James, "Great Men, Great Thoughts and Their Environment," *Atlantic Monthly* 46 (1880): 441–459.
6. Tim R. Davis and Fred Luthans, "Leadership Reexamined: A Behavioral Approach," *Academy of Management Review* 4, no. 2 (1979): 237–248, 239.
7. Arnold Bakker and Wilmar Schaufeli, "Positive Organizational Behavior: Engaged Employees in Flourishing Organizations," *Journal of Organizational Behavior* 29, no. 2 (2008): 147–54.
8. Svafa Grönfeldt and Judith Strother, *Service Leadership: The Quest for Competitive Advantage* (Thousand Oaks, CA: Sage Publication, 2006), 105.
9. David L. Bradford and Allan R. Cohen, "The Postheroic Leader," *Training and Development Journal* 38, no. 1 (1984): 40–49.

CHAPTER 1

LEADERSHIP THEORIES

Traditional and Transformational

Management is efficiency in climbing the ladder of success;
leadership determines whether the ladder is leaning against the right wall.
—*Stephen R. Covey*[1]

As librarians, we see the deluge of literature on management and leadership, whether scholarly, practical, or popular, that is published year after year. There is usually one book title that is on everyone's lips (whether or not it is on their minds is another matter) for a few months. It may even be inculcated into organizational training so that everyone can be indoctrinated into the new routine and the latest jargon until the next management fad comes along to replace it. Often the advice passed on is nothing new or innovative; it's merely framed in a new context for an emerging situation or with new buzzwords.

That said, there are a number of seminal works on leadership that are universal in perspective and provide a critical foundation upon which this book is built. While the ideas and models they present are diverse and may seem to be mutually exclusive or even, at times, conflicting, facets of them complement each other and provide value in framing the service leadership model and discussion of its implications for libraries.

MANAGEMENT VS. LEADERSHIP

Leadership has a multitude of definitions, both in the various literatures and in practice, framed by personal experience, by relationships, and by individuals known through experience, the media, or history. This is quite aside from the distinctions between management and leadership, which are sometimes—and quite incorrectly—used synonymously. Management is often defined through a specific title, office, or position of authority and those who have held them. In this way, the manager or administrator is called a leader, someone who directs subordinates with the authority invested in the position. Managers are either promoted or hired; status is bestowed as a king is crowned. Leadership may be confused with an authoritarian model focusing on the power distance between leader and follower: as with a king, a president, or a general and their subjects.

As a result of this confusion, it is necessary to understand the difference between a manager and a leader and why this difference is significant. It is also important to stress that good managers can also be good leaders and that many leaders were at one time managers. The director of an organization—the library for our purposes—is by no means the only leader, although it is not uncommon for leadership to be recognized only in those with a management title. However, a manager and a leader are definitely not the same; each has its own distinct roles, which may be mutually exclusive, and in light of the leadership issues that libraries have and will continue to face, a distinction must be made.

Warren Bennis, widely regarded as a pioneer of the contemporary field of leadership studies, compares the attributes of a manager and a leader to highlight the difference between the two:

- The manager administers; the leader innovates.
- The manager is a copy; the leader is the original.
- The manager maintains; the leader develops.
- The manager focuses on systems and structure; the leader focuses on people.
- The manager relies on control; the leader inspires trust.
- The manager has a short-range view; the leader has a long-range perspective.
- The manager asks how and when; the leader asks what and why.
- The manager has his or her eye always on the bottom line; the leader's eye is on the horizon.
- The manager imitates; the leader originates.
- The manager accepts the status quo; the leader challenges it.
- The manager does things right; the leader does the right thing.[2]

What Bennis stresses in his comparison is that a manager tends to control the situation by focusing attention on the process of completing a task which was defined externally or handed down by the leader (or that person at the top of the organizational chart). Leaders, on the other hand, project the vision of a library's mission and how this mission may be achieved, carrying this message to everyone connected to the library. Without leaders, the library would be adrift without a strategy, and without managers, the strategic plan could not be implemented. As a result, libraries are increasingly facing a crisis of effective leadership in which managers are trying to lead without either the skills or vision to be effective leaders. Think back to people with positional authority in your library; were they visionaries or micromanagers and taskmasters? If you answered the latter, then you have a manager in a leadership position, and as a result, the typical leadership in your library may tend to be hierarchical, task-based, and archaic.

Leadership can also be observed at an organizational level. This is often defined by the success of a company, measured by stock value or sales in dollars (or yen, lira, etc.). IBM, Ritz-Carlton, Southwest Airlines, Apple, and Starbucks may have been considered leaders in their field at any specific time. In these business environments, the leadership values have been adopted by the organization and become part of its culture. In this way, the organization is peopled by leaders and tends to stand out in its field. Metrics used in a corporate environment are less relevant to service organizations, particularly those with a public or educational mission such as libraries. However, there are ways to measure success; they just tend to be less tangible and short term.

WHAT IS LEADERSHIP?

This book will look at leadership in terms of the capacity to lead, using the significance of "to guide on a way, especially by *going in advance*."[3] In this case, advance means being the first to do something, a pioneer. It is as essential a component of leadership as guiding others to follow a path, and perhaps more so, because so much significance is placed on choosing the direction and the modeling of certain behaviors. We are focusing on leadership in terms of forging a new path, rather than following the one that has gone before or doing what is expected by others. It assumes that an individual has strength of purpose and vision to go forward regardless of whether one is leading the pack or following those in authority; in fact, it requires that a leader challenge the status quo and seek the less traveled path. It looks at leadership in the larger context, not merely at the local organization or department.

This flies in the face of the traditional perception, asserted by Emmanuel Gobillot in *Follow the Leader*, that having followers is the necessary definition of leadership.[4] Certainly, he goes on to indicate that great leaders have great followers and describes what that looks like. This is a traditional view of leadership, and it raises the chicken-or-egg dilemma: If a leader is defined by his or her followers (and just by having followers), then how does one become a leader except by having followers? In addition, we are not looking at positional authority as an indicator of leadership; in many cases, that is also a case of follow the leader, with middle and even upper management doing what the individual at the top of the pyramid wants or what they think he or she wants. This is NOT the view of leadership discussed here. To illustrate what leading is, according to this book, we provide a couple of examples. Joseph Nye discusses the process of *Time* magazine's editorial board choosing the most important person of the century:

> They narrowed the list to Churchill, Franklin D. Roosevelt, Mahatma Gandhi and Albert Einstein. They picked Einstein as the person whose extraordinary creativity had the greatest impact on the age, but, unlike the others, Einstein was not a leader . . . He had spent a lifetime flaunting authority and going his own way and regarded it as ironic that he should become an authority.[5]

Nye's use of *leader* and *authority* seems, on the surface, to undermine the argument. However, it illustrates a fundamental aspect of leadership that we are trying to emphasize: leadership is making those decisions, those actions that are true to the individual's purpose, and doing so at times in spite of expectations and traditional roles. The second example is more recent, more relevant, and less prepossessing: Admiral McRaven was recently selected as president of the University of Texas (UT) System. Prior to this distinction, he gave a commencement speech that has gone viral because it speaks to purpose in living and leading. He illustrated UT's slogan, "What Starts Here Changes the World," with lessons from his own life, in fact from his U.S. Navy SEALs training. He emphasizes the significance of service and that leadership in service sometimes requires that an individual make the right decision in times of hardship and in the absence of either followers or leaders.[6]

LEADERSHIP THEORIES

There are as many definitions for the term *leadership* as there are leadership theories.[7] The question of what makes a leader has been explored for centuries, and the plethora of meanings and theories is largely due to the increased interest in leaders and leadership over the past 200 years and how leadership is often conflated with power. Treatises on and definitions of leadership show up in nearly every discipline but are largely concentrated in public administration or political science, military history, management, psychology, and sociology. Early theorists, such as Thomas Carlyle and Francis Galton, limited their focus on the leader's traits and how these were different from those they lead, contributing to the corpus of leadership theories known as "Great Man" theories. Gradually leadership theorists, such as Hersey, Blanchard, Bird, and Mann, began to cast a wider net in their research to include an array of variables such as task, relationship, and behavioral elements that affect a leader's ability to be successful. These theories differed from many contemporary leadership theories, such as Service Leadership, because they divorced the leader's traits from the situation. They argued that the leader's individual traits were not persistent over time, and as a result, individuals could be effective leaders in a certain situation but not in others.

Theories on leadership have evolved, largely varying in where they postulate leadership comes from. Many traditional leadership theories focus on the leader as a singular figure and her actions while leading. The great man theories and trait theories both address leadership in terms of the inherent qualities of the leader. Behavioral theories are more focused on the actions of the leader, which are easier to discern and define than traits. Contingency theory, or situational leadership, is based on the perspective that the leader modifies her style or actions in response to the situation. Participative and transactional leadership still assume a hierarchical relationship, but the interaction between leader and follower is defined by specific expectations for each role, with the power residing with the leader. Although the early leadership theories divorced the leader's traits from the situation, their focus remained on the person who had positional authority. However, they lacked an examination of the relationship between leader and follower and what, if any, leadership role the follower had. One such leadership theory style that took into consideration upward feedback for decision-making was participative theory, more commonly called shared leadership theory. This theory, which grew out of the human relations movement of the 1920s, encouraged employees to voice their opinions and be a part of the decision-making process. It was hoped that this participative input would improve the employees' and leaders' perceptions of each other while helping both to understand the overall organization. It was also hoped that this participative input would help employees feel more pertinent and loyal not only to the decision but also to the organization. In spite of this participatory advancement, in libraries as in all other organizations, this input could backfire when employees either perceived that their director was paying lip service to their opinions but had already made a decision or that their voice was not being heard. This adverse reaction can having damning effects on the morale of the organization and could create a change-resistant organizational culture.

This book will examine the theories that focus on the relationship between the leader and the follower in a more collaborative and equitable way—leadership without assuming power distance, authority, or subordination.

Leadership can be viewed from a number of different perspectives. Northouse, for example, discusses the various perspectives on leadership as a trait, ability, skill, behavior (focus on action), and relationship (leaders are focused on the performance of the group and its members).[8]

Northouse eloquently explains these five perspectives in detail:

- "Defining leadership as a trait means that each individual brings to the table certain inherent qualities that influence the way he or she leads. Some leaders are confident, some are decisive, and still others are outgoing and sociable. Saying that leadership is a trait placed a great deal of emphasis on the leader and on the leader's special gifts. It follows the often-expressed belief that 'leaders are born, not made. . . .

- Leadership is also conceptualized as an ability. A person who has leadership ability is able to be a leader—that is, has the capacity to lead. While the term 'ability' frequently refers to a natural capacity, ability can be acquired. For example, some people are naturally good at public speaking, while others rehearse to become comfortable speaking in public . . . In leadership, some people have the natural ability to lead, while others develop their leadership abilities through hard work and practice. . . .

- Conceptualized as a skill, leadership is a *competency* developed to accomplish a task effectively. Skilled leaders are competent people who know the means and methods for carrying out their responsibilities . . . In short, skilled leaders are competent—they know what they need to do and they know how to do it. Describing leadership as a skill makes leadership available to everyone because skills are competencies that people can learn or develop. . . .

- Leadership is also a behavior. It is *what leaders do* when they are in a leadership role. The behavioral dimension is concerned with how leaders act toward others in various situations. Unlike traits, abilities, and skills, leadership behaviors are observable. When someone leads, we see that person's leadership behavior. Research on leadership has shown that leaders engage primarily in two kinds of general behaviors: *task behaviors* and *process behaviors*. Task behaviors are used by leaders to get the job done (e.g., they prepare an agenda for a meeting). Process behaviors are used by leaders to help people feel comfortable with other group members and at ease in the situations in which they find themselves (e.g., they help individuals in a group to feel included). Since leadership requires both task and process behaviors, the challenge for leaders is to know the best way to combine them in their efforts to reach a goal.

- Another, and somewhat unusual, way to think about leadership is as a *relationship*. From this perspective, leadership is centered in the communication between leaders and followers rather than on the unique qualities of the leader. Thought of as a relationship, leadership becomes a process of collaboration that occurs between leaders and followers. A leader affects and is affected by followers, and both leader and followers are affected in turn by the situation that surrounds them. This approach emphasizes that leadership is not a linear one-way event, but rather an interactive event. In traditional leadership, authority is often top down; in the interactive type of leadership, authority and influence are shared. When leadership is defined in this manner, it becomes available to everyone. It is not restricted to the formally designated leader in a group."[9]

Leadership is about the development of those behaviors, abilities, and skills; it is about being the first to take an action because it is the right thing to do, not because there is prestige in being first and not because there is an assumption that others will follow. Leadership is each of these facets: a trait, ability, skill, behavior, and relationship. It is consistent with Lueneburger's assertion that cultures of purpose are composed of "three sets of building blocks that depend on and influence each other": competencies, traits, and cultural attributes.[10] Each informs the others, and leadership can be taught, although the most effective lessons are in life rather than in the classroom. Leadership can be learned, but only if an individual is willing and self-aware. These qualities will be discussed in more detail in later chapters.

Transformational Leadership

James MacGregor Burns is credited with introducing the concept of transformational leadership, which is largely considered the modern definition of leadership. He referred to it as transforming leadership in that it is literally predicated on a change or paradigm shift. He made the distinction from the traditional view of transactional leadership, defined as a relationship based on the exchange of valued things, a kind of quid pro quo or even business-based foundation. Conversely, transforming leadership "occurs when one or more persons *engage* with others in such a way that the leaders and followers raise one another to higher levels of motivation and morality."[11] Transforming leadership assumes a nontangible investment in others with no specific expectation of personal return on investment. This was significantly different than previous leadership theories because the transformational approach changed the traditional way employees and leaders perceived each other's role. The leaders were no longer telling the employees what the organization needed to do, and the employees were no longer following their leaders blindly. The employees now had the opportunity to give the leader feedback and ask questions while making suggestions about how to achieve the organizational goal. This fluid form of communication between leader and follower helps to raise awareness about the importance of organizational goals and the various ways in which it achieves these goals. Transformational leadership differs from transactional leadership theory by being proactive and engaging employees in the success of the organization, by motivating them to consider the organization's interests above their own self-interest. Transactional leaders, on the other hand, are responsive to situations, not proactive, and tend to motivate or demotivate their employees by appealing to their own self-interest. They may be passive and engage their employees by offering rewards and penalties, such as bigger offices, promotions/demotions, and monetary compensation, or threatening penalties in an effort to influence the work and loyalty of their employees.

Burns believed that the United States was facing a leadership crisis[12] and developed a transformational leadership theory that continued to focus on the critical relationship between leader and follower. Bernard Bass extended this model, examining how to advance the organization by developing an organizational culture that rested on a high level of morale and motivation. This high level of morale and motivation could only be achieved if there was a strong and equal exchange of communication between the leader and the followers. Everyone needed to understand and be aware of the important tasks the organization needed to accomplish while keeping in mind the organization's values.

Morality plays a major role in transforming leadership and in relationships upon which it is based. "Transforming leadership ultimately becomes *moral* in that it raises the level of human conduct and ethical aspiration of both leader and led, and thus it has a transforming effect on both."[13] The morality that Burn's speaks of is not based on a specific philosophical, religious, or sociopolitical platform; morality in leadership refers to a shared understanding and shared commitment. Burns asserts that it "emerges from, and always returns to, the fundamental wants and needs, aspirations and values of the followers,"[14] through which a larger social change can be realized. This concept has informed later theories, founded upon the aspects of relationship-building and shared commitment; in the context of service leadership and servant leadership, the purpose is service to others.

Bass and Avolio expanded on Burns' premise and provided a framework for what they called transformational leadership, as follows:

1. Idealized influence attends to the concept of modeling behavior that inspires trust and promotes mutual respect. It also speaks to ideals or a shared morality.
2. Inspirational motivation addresses the ability to communicate meaning and purpose to an individual and an organization. This includes both the vision and the ability to articulate that vision in a compelling way.
3. Intellectual stimulation promotes individual and organizational development, challenging the norm and encouraging this behavior in others. Creativity and risk-taking are evidence of this factor.
4. Individualized consideration describes the investment that is made in each person in the organization, in terms of understanding their needs and wants, their strengths and weaknesses. It is indicated in listening and community.[15]

Kouzes and Posner began their examination of leadership by first asking new and experienced leaders how leadership has changed over time. They summarized their findings indicating that "the fundamentals of leadership are the same today as they were in the 1980s, and they've probably been the same for centuries. Yet the leaders were quick to add that while the *content* of leadership has not changed, the *context* has—and, in some cases, it has changed dramatically."[16] Taking this knowledge into consideration, Kouzes and Posner began their leadership research by defining leaders as people who "mobilize others to want to get extraordinary things done in organizations."[17] This is significant because it deals with influence rather than positional authority and starts with the assumption that anyone can be a leader, regardless of their status or rank. What matters, however, is the motivating connection to others in the organization. Kouzes and Posner built on this concept by developing their five practices of exemplary leadership, each of which elaborated on what motivates a leader to commitments and behaviors:

1. *Model the Way* encourages leaders to act and behave the same way they encourage their employees to act and behave. Not only does this encompass the values the organization promotes but also encompasses both personal values and the way in which those values influence behavior in terms of actions or words. Leaders must clarify their personal values, find their voice, and align their actions with the shared values of the organization.
2. *Inspire Shared Vision* addresses the collaborative process of "imagining exciting and ennobling possibilities . . . by appealing to shared aspirations so that everyone in the organization understands and works toward these goals."
3. *Challenge the Process* urges the rejection of complacency and "the way we have always done it." It seeks different and innovative ways to change, grow, and improve the organization. It also advocates risk-taking and experimentation to progress, learn, and develop.
4. *Enable Others to Act* focuses on the role of empowering others and relationship-building for purposes of collaboration and trust.
5. *Encourage the Heart,* the most uncommonly seen in leadership roles, is the positive reinforcement and encouragement involved in recognizing performance and individual contributions, which ultimately celebrates the use of the organization's values.[18]

Charismatic Leadership, initially postulated by House, appears at first to be a trait-based theory. He defined it as a dominant, strong desire to influence others, a self-confident and strong sense of one's own moral values. It was further developed by Conger and Kanungo who, extending it beyond a trait-based model, identified several behaviors that can be developed by individuals and organizations alike:

1. Vision and articulation, similar to inspirational motivation, addresses the ability to realize and convey meaning and mission.
2. Sensitivity to the environment can be seen in both the ability to identify and assess environmental factors that may impact the organization.
3. Sensitivity to member needs is the sincere concern for others, their needs, and their well-being.
4. Personal risk-taking describes behaviors for the good of the organization that may come at a personal expense.
5. Performing unconventional behavior, similar to challenging the process and building on personal risk taking, addresses the revolutionary aspect of leadership that it is not necessary to follow what has always been done or what everyone else does.[19]

Goleman et al. explored the place of emotion in leadership, arguing that "The fundamental task of leaders . . . is to prime good feeling in those they lead."[20] They go on to say that "being intelligent about emotions—matters so much for leadership success."[21] Goleman outlines four emotional intelligence domains:

1. Self-awareness includes emotional self-awareness, accurate self-assessment, and self-confidence.
2. Self-regulation is characterized by emotional self-control, transparency, adaptability, achievement, initiative, and optimism.
3. Social skill encompasses empathy, organizational awareness, and service.
4. Relationship management addresses inspiring leadership, influencing and developing others, catalyzing change, managing conflict, building bonds, teamwork, and collaboration.[22]

These competencies are not necessarily only individually oriented; they can be developed at the organizational level. They are invariably embedded in the purpose and standards of the organization and influence the overall culture and success of the organization.

Authentic and Ethical Leadership

Authentic leadership, ironically, has been hard to define, though many have tried. Bill George writes that "leadership is authenticity, not style."[23] He goes on to describe the five dimensions of authentic leaders:

1. Understanding their purpose, which is related to their morality but also to their passion.
2. Practicing solid values addresses aligning behavior with morality.
3. Leading with heart advocates practicing compassion.
4. Practicing connected relationships demonstrates a focus on community and collaboration.
5. Demonstrating self-discipline illustrates modeling behavior that is consistent with morality.[24]

Interestingly, the need for authenticity is not always articulated in leadership models. Ethical leadership, similar to authentic leadership, is involved in leading in a manner that respects the rights and dignity of others. There is growing interest in this area, particularly within the business and corporate arena and largely due to financial scandals. Trevino looks at leadership from an ethical perspective, similar to the concept of morality that Burns espoused. In this case, there is a dichotomy to her model: ethical behavior as an individual as well as ethical behavior as a manager responsible for directing others' behavior.[25] Individual moral behavior is indicated by honesty, integrity, trust, and openness; concern for people and for personal morality; and values-based and fair decision-making. The moral behavior of a manager is typified by role modeling (visible ethical action) and holding people accountable for ethical conduct. It communicates and conveys an "ethics/values" message.

Lueneburger also underscores the importance of a shared morality, defining a culture of purpose as "a shared intent with impact beyond the organization itself. Because it captures an ideal that goes beyond . . . any other measure of whether you are doing things right. A purpose, instead, is a pledge to the right things."[26]

Northouse distills many of the major leadership theories down to five fundamental and elegantly simple ethical principles, "the origins of which can be traced back to Aristotle:"[27]

1. Respect others;
2. Serve others;
3. Show justice;
4. Manifest honesty; and
5. Build community.[28]

These tenets are essentially the Golden Rule framed for the organizational context. Servant leadership is also closely related to this principle and is comparable to authentic leadership and transformational leadership, but it will be discussed in depth in the next chapter, particularly as it contributes to service leadership.

NOTES

1. Stephen R. Covey, *The 7 Habits of Highly Effective People: Powerful Lessons in Personal Change* (New York, NY: Free Press, 2004), 101.

2. Warren Bennis, *On Becoming a Leader,* (New York: Perseus Books, 2009), 42.

3. Merriam-Webster Online, www.merriam-webster.com.

4. Emmanuel Gobillot, *Follow the Leader: The One Thing Great Leaders Have That Great Followers Want* (Philadelphia, PA: Kogan Page Publishers, 2013).

5. Joseph S. Nye, *The Powers to Lead* (New York, NY: Oxford University Press, 2008), 16–17.

6. The University of Texas at Austin, "Adm. McRaven Urges Graduates to Find Courage to Change the World," May 16, 2014, www.utexas.edu/news/2014/05/16/admiral-mcraven-commencement-speech.

7. Donald E. Riggs, "The Crisis and Opportunities in Library Leadership," *Journal of Library Leadership* 32, no. 3/4 (2011): 5–17.

8. Peter G. Northouse, *Introduction to Leadership: Concepts and Practice* (Thousand Oaks, CA: Sage Publications, 2009), 2.

9. Ibid., 2–3.

10. Christoph Lueneburger, *A Culture of Purpose: How to Choose the Right People and Make the Right People Choose You* (San Francisco, CA: Jossey-Bass, 2014).

11. James MacGregor Burns, *Leadership* (New York, NY: Harper & Row, 1978), 20.

12. Ibid., 1.

13. Ibid., 20.

14. Ibid., 4.

15. Bernard M. Bass and Bruce J. Avolio, "Transformational Leadership and Organizational Culture," *Public Administration Quarterly* 17, no.1 (1993): 112.

16. James M. Kouzes and Barry Z. Posner, *The Leadership Challenge,* 3rd ed. (San Francisco, CA: Jossey-Bass, 2002), xviii.

17. Ibid., xvii.

18. Ibid., 14–20.

19. Jay A. Conger and Rabindra N. Kanungo, "Toward a Behavioral Theory of Charismatic Leadership in Organizational Settings," *The Academy of Management Review* 12, no. 4 (1987): 637–647.

20. D. Goleman, R. Boyatzis, and A. McKee, *Primal Leadership: Realizing the Power of Emotional Intelligence* (Boston, MA: Harvard Business School Press, 2002), ix.

21. Ibid.

22. Ibid., 30.

23. Bill George, *Authentic Leadership: Rediscovering the Secrets to Creating Lasting Value* (San Francisco, CA.: Jossey-Bass, 2003), 11.

24. Ibid., 18.

25. Linda K. Trevino, *Ethical Leadership: Creating an Ethical Culture,* 2005, www.scu.edu/ethics/practicing/focusareas/business/conference/presentations/Trevino.ppt.

26. Christoph Lueneburger, *A Culture of Purpose: How to Choose the Right People and Make the Right People Choose You* (San Francisco, CA: Jossey-Bass, 2014).

27. Peter G. Northouse, *Leadership: Theory and Practice* (Thousand Oaks, CA: Sage Publications, 2010), 386.

28. Ibid.

CHAPTER 2

SERVICE LEADERSHIP AND ITS PARADIGM IN LIBRARIES

> Control is not leadership; management is not leadership; leadership is leadership. If you seek to lead, invest at least 50% of your time in leading yourself—your own purpose, ethics, principles, motivation, conduct.
> —*Dee Hock*[1]

Service leadership in libraries is derived, in some measure, from Robert Greenleaf's leadership philosophy of servant leadership, although it also is informed by aspects of other leadership models. Greenleaf defines a leader as a person who is a servant first. But, the term *servant*, meaning an individual attending to the needs of others, or in a librarian's case, the library user patron, often leaves a bad taste in the mouths' of leaders. Because the term is often linked with more altruistic philosophies, it may be disregarded in academic settings, particularly with the growing culture of accountability and the application of business models in higher education.

SERVANT LEADERSHIP

Servant leadership is built on transformational leadership as well as on ethical or authentic leadership, with altruism at its core: The disparity between servant leaders and transformational leaders is that servant leaders make a priority of "selecting the needs of others and serving others as the leader's main aim, whereas transformational leaders aim to align their own and others' interests with the good of the group, organization, or society . . ."[2] The fundamental tenet of servant leadership, as articulated by Greenleaf and reiterated by scholars in the field, is that "The servant-leader *is* servant first . . . It begins with the natural feeling that one wants to serve, to serve *first*."[3] This is consistent with the concept of "to guide by going in advance"—that the motivation or inspiration is not to lead as if at the head of some parade but to pioneer. Some seek to serve and are chosen to lead. Through their own values and motivation, through their desire to maintain integrity and help others—there are times when an individual may walk the path alone and there are times when they may look behind them, finding that there are those who follow their example. " . . . Greenleaf is saying that leadership is a special case of service, he is not saying that service is a special case of leadership. . . . As I understand him, he is not asking, 'What service can you render as a leader?' but rather 'What leadership can you exercise as a servant?'"[4] Additionally "servant leadership shares similar key characteristics with authentic leadership in that both explicitly recognize the importance of positive moral perspective, self-awareness, self-regulation (i.e., authentic behavior), positive modeling, and a focus on follower development . . ."[5]

Intriguingly, there is some reticence within librarianship to identify servant leadership as a valuable model. Perhaps it is the seeming paradoxical nature of servant-leadership, that it is through service that one leads, or because librarians have long struggled to establish their professionalism and so they see any connection with *servant* as undermining these efforts, as pejorative in a way. However, the aspects of servant leadership, as defined by Greenleaf, are highly relevant to the profession:

1. Listening
2. Empathy
3. Healing
4. Awareness
5. Persuasion
6. Conceptualization
7. Foresight
8. Stewardship
9. Commitment to the growth of people
10. Building community[6]

Servant leadership has also been widely identified with spiritual and philanthropic efforts, though less with educational and academic ones such as libraries. Greenleaf's philosophy thoroughly aligns with libraries, their role as a public good, and their mission and commitment to service.

DEFINING SERVICE

Before discussing what service leadership is, one must first understand what service is and the context of the definition. Historically, service has been defined in a variety of ways ranging from the general, such as the primary function of an entire profession or practice, to the specific, focusing on the value created by a particular effort or function. For example, service can be "economic activities that produce time, place, form, or psychological utilities. Services are acts, deeds, or performances that are intangible."[7] Quinn et al., define service more descriptively, stating that service activities "include[s] all economic activities whose output is not a physical product or construction, is generally consumed at the time it is produced, and provides added value in forms (such as convenience, amusement, timelines, comfort, or health) that are essentially intangible concerns of its first purchaser."[8]

Leonard Berry, largely considered the father of the service quality movement, defines service from a business perspective and from his many examples indicates that the definition of service is also very contextual. He asserts that ". . . customers are the sole judge of service quality. Customers assess service by comparing the service they receive (perceptions) with the service they desire (expectations)."[9] That said, Berry puts service at the center of an organization's purpose, indicating that strategy, planning, and process should all evolve from that purpose.

Grönfeldt and Strother refer to service as customer service, but the relationship in this sense is still fundamentally transactional. They believe that service has different characteristics from goods or tangible products, which are specific objects manufactured at one time and then sold or used later. In contrast, service is intangible. It is created and consumed simultaneously (or nearly simultaneously). This suggests that service cannot be stocked or easily demonstrated beforehand.[10] The service definition proposed by Grönfeldt and Strother assumes a business or corporate environment, and the motivation for service in this environment is distinct from the concept of service in the nonprofit sector. Their definition assumes a fundamental economic authority, whereas public organizations are generally governed through political compliance.[11] The fundamental mission of government entities, academic institutions, and nonprofit organizations is service to the public: "The point is that service, service to people or service to a cause, is at the heart of the reason for being of all of these organizations."[12]

The concept of the public good addresses the commitment that these organizations have to serve their constituencies— not for profit, not to promote themselves, and not to perpetuate their existence—but rather to fill the needs of others; fundamentally, their mission is to serve. This mission affords them a unique relationship with their customers or patrons: "Nonprofit organizations, especially public benefit organizations, exist and are granted specific privileges (as noted above) with the explicit understanding that they are committed in some way to serve the public good."[13] The philosophy and commitment to service extends, not only to the customer or patron, but to employees and colleagues within the organization. It is a matter of modeling the service ethic at all levels and in all relationships, ultimately permeating the organization: ". . . the willingness of managers and leaders to see themselves as servants of others may be crucial to focusing others in an organization on the organization's commitment to serve."[14]

In other words, by serving employees and colleagues, an organization is providing better service to its patrons. Conversely, in a business environment in which the relationship may be transactional and the motivation monetary, this value may also drive the organization. Many assume that management books tend to describe businesses and for-profit organizations because that audience is large, commercially driven, and focused on money. While that may be, it could also be posited that companies, as opposed to academic institutions or government agencies, are more plugged into their patrons (those they serve) and are asking the right questions and aligning their purpose with their patron's needs and desires.

Similar to corporate entities who are generally selling something, service organizations, specifically libraries, must have something to offer the public at large. Through competence and objectivity, they provide information to their patrons, enabling them to educate themselves, address problems, make better decisions, and contribute to the world, ultimately perpetuating the public good.

One drawback to this concept of a public good is related to the intangibility of service and the inherent lack of transaction or valuing of the service:

> A profession that inherently believes that it is a "public good" does not feel the need to demonstrate outcomes and articulate impact. There is a deeply held and tacit assumption that the "good" is widely recognized and the value of library service is universally appreciated. In the current environment of competition and of questioning every assumption, this deeply held value results in resistance to change and resistance to continuous assessment.[15]

In the context of libraries and other public service organizations, "a commitment to service should be manifest in those managers making practical and strategic choices that give precedence to fulfilling the mission of their organization over possibilities for advancing their own status and careers."[16] In other words, the modeling of service as a value should manifest in all activities and in all roles within the organization. While any individual can be a service leader or practice principles of service leadership, this service orientation is most effective when modeled by those with managerial responsibilities or supervisory authority.

Service leadership is more than a leadership theory; it is a cultural mindset that empowers all library employees to extend their customer service philosophy so that it can develop, becoming an organizational practice and cultural value. Strother and Grönfeldt address service leadership from a business perspective, stating:

> A service leadership mindset of an entire organization will consider every employee-customer encounter to be an invaluable opportunity to improve customer service and engender customer loyalty. Under these conditions,

SERVICE LEADERSHIP IN PRACTICE

Yet They Serve . . . Leadership isn't an are-you-aren't-you proposition: it is really a continuum in multiple dimensions where individuals are more or less effective at different facets. That said, there are those rare individuals who are the entire package; more common are those who, in a holistic sense, are successful as leaders. Looking back, for as many managers and administrators as we have worked under or with or had the opportunity to be part of their organization, there is only one who stands out as a true servant leader and his leadership was certainly recognized on many levels and in many venues: Robert M. Gates, the former Secretary of Defense, director of the CIA and, in the role with which I am most familiar, president of Texas A&M University. His resume is long and distinguished but his own words exemplify the commitment of those who serve:

> Each one in public service has his or her own story—and motives. But I believe, if you scratch deeply enough, you will find that those who serve—no matter how outwardly tough or jaded or egotistical—are, in their heart of hearts, romantics and idealists. And optimists. We actually believe we can make a difference, that we can make the lives of others better, that we can make a positive difference in the life of the greatest country in the history of the world—in President Lincoln's words, 'the last, best, hope of earth.' Public servants are people willing to make sacrifices in the present for the future good—people who believe, to paraphrase Walter Lippmann, that we must plant trees that we may never get to sit under. They include those of my generation, who heard President Kennedy challenge us nearly 47 years ago, "Ask not what your country can do for you, but what you can do for your country." And people of a later generation heard this president, George H. W. Bush, affirm that "Public service is a noble calling.[17]

Gates was reluctant to leave Texas A&M, but in a message to all employees, he explained that he had been called to serve and must go do his duty.

every individual takes responsibility and pride in creating or protecting the organization's leading position in service quality or in designated markets by carefully observing and communicating customer needs throughout the organization.[18]

In order to achieve a service leadership model throughout an organization, the leader who may or may not have positional authority, must embody the service leadership mindset by introducing the service leadership model into an organization's culture through its mission statement and subsequent actions. However, there a number of steps that must be taken in order to achieve this goal:

1. The individual, through self-reflection, must become aware of who she is, what she believes in, what her values are, and how all of these factors motivate her to react.
2. After this self-reflection, the individual must be true, honest, and committed to behaving and reacting the same way in the same or similar situations.
3. The individual, after self-reflection, must become conscious of how their values and beliefs affect how they view and understand the people they work with and their patrons. They must understand that people have different opinions and that these opinions must be respected and considered in order for there to be social justice.
4. Following the individual self-reflection stage, the individual as leader must empower his team to be the best organization it can be, trusting in their professional experience.
5. Once the team's professional experience has been assessed, the group must come together to identify the organization's purpose and goals so that the organization has one mission statement that everyone understands and models.

Each individual needs to recognize that all employees, regardless of their positions, are essential to the organization. It is the employees who possess the intellectual capital and deliver efficient and effective service to their customers or patrons. These employees offer their customers unique service that is difficult to imitate through outsourcing.[19] Individuals can model the values of service leadership and raise awareness in the organization, making localized changes. However, it is extremely difficult for the service leadership mindset to infiltrate the organizational culture without a leader who has positional authority. It is necessary for a leader high enough within the management hierarchy to influence employees to believe in, support, and promote the service leadership model so that everyone inside and outside of the business understands and supports the plan. Consequently, the organizational culture rests on the values created and communicated by the company president or organization executive and her administrative team. The key is that service leadership needs to go beyond wishing that the company's mission is followed; individuals must make the mission true by leading by example.[20] A service leader must not only communicate these values every day but embody these values consistently in everything that she does.

LEARNING ORGANIZATION

Libraries are the ultimate learning organization; their mission is to educate and empower people with information. They put this value into practice through critical inquiry and learning in their everyday work.

In spite of the increasing number of theories advocating communication flow between the employee and leader, historically, there was the underlying premise that the final decision-making remained in the hands of the person with positional authority. Gradually, there was a shift as theories began to surface around collective leadership and teaming in which leadership applied to all employees within an organization and was meant to foster a leadership mind-set for a whole organization.[21] One of the first leadership theorists to promote collective leadership was Peter Senge. Senge gradually moved beyond the positional authoritarian definition of a leader and considered the importance of fostering leadership at all levels of an organization, not just the top echelon. During this "age of empowerment," there was recognition that it is disempowering and demotivating for employees within an organization to believe that only top management can cause significant change.[22] Senge states that:

> Human beings are designed for learning. No one has to teach an infant to walk, or talk, or master the spatial relationships needed to stack eight building blocks that don't topple. Children come fully equipped with an insatiable drive to explore and experiment. Unfortunately, the primary institutions of our society are oriented predominantly toward controlling rather than learning, rewarding individuals for performing for others rather than for cultivating their natural curiosity and impulse to learn.[23]

Cultivation of learning creates superior performance by the employee and for the organization, which can only be achieved if an employee is empowered, self-directed, and allowed to make mistakes and to learn from them. Senge believes that organizations can no longer afford to continue having only their leaders "learn for the organization." This is because it is no longer possible for leaders with positional authority to "figure it out at the top" and then pass this vision down to the employees to implement. The success of the organization depends on giving "way to integrated thinking and acting at all levels."[24] In order to create a learning organization, Senge believed that there are five leadership learning disciplines, the foundations of which are built on the ethics, ideas, and values of the learning organization.

Senge's model for organizational leadership also addresses the organization as a leader within its sector or industry and discusses how to lead such an organization. Senge's vision of leadership, within the context of the learning organization, is similar to that of the model advocated herein and in both service and servant leadership, as "designers, stewards, and teachers."[25] He goes on to enumerate five principles or disciplines that are the foundations of the learning organization and asserts that a discipline is a "developmental path for acquiring certain skills or competencies," thus underscoring the premise that leadership is a skill and can be learned:

1. Systems thinking is the fundamental recognition that there is no such thing as a closed system, that there are various inputs and outputs that may occur at various stages. It is the ability to see the big picture or both the forest and the trees.

2. Personal mastery is the commitment to the process of learning. This is the foundation of several other theories, such as Total Quality Management (TQM), and movements, such as the recent focus on assessment. An organization is the sum of employee's performance or individual learning. A learning organization recognizes that the component most significant to organizational success is individual learning.

3. Mental models refer to the perspectives or assumptions held by both individuals and by organizations; weltanschauung is a similar concept, referring to the framework through which individuals view the world. A learning organization will challenge assumptions and encourage individuals to challenge their own.

4. Shared vision is critical because it provides both a context and an incentive for learning. It builds on the promise and commitment of everyone within the organization and, as such, is more likely to succeed and be sustained.

5. Team learning is the culmination of the individual learning and the realization that the whole is greater than the sum of the parts; some would call it synergy (although it is much overused).[26]

The concept of the learning organization primarily informs sustainability and adaptability—in other words, how to effectively and successfully deal with change. Since change is not only a fact of life for libraries but a principal driver, these are primary considerations and principles that can successfully inform leadership in libraries.

LEADERSHIP IN LIBRARIES

Today, we live in a fast-paced environment in which all leaders within any organization are forced to examine and reexamine how their organization can stay relevant, continue to meet the changing needs of their patrons, and sustain their efforts. This competitive priority is as true for libraries as it is for companies, but libraries have the added problem of a lack of attention to effective leadership. In the early 1980s, Riggs reported that, although administration and management in librarianship were well-covered in the literature, there was a noticeable scarcity of material on library leadership.[27] The reason for this scarcity was that most of the leadership literature dealing with libraries was not only redundant but it actually revolved around administration and management issues and not true leadership issues. Riggs was particularly concerned about this confusion over the difference between leadership and administration and management,[28] which he believed caused librarians to be confused about what true leadership in the profession was since "the sum of the highest development of each (administration and management) does not add up to leadership."[29]

Increasing the confusion about leadership in the library science profession was the lack of formal library science leadership education in degree-granting library and information science (LIS) programs. Library Science programs teach classes in library administration or management but do not teach true library leadership.[30] This perpetuates the leadership problem in libraries because it reinforces a misunderstanding between what a library manager is and does versus a library leader. This creates an environment where some library leaders may not be library leaders at all but rather managers under the disguise of a leader.

This leadership problem is further exacerbated by the changing demographics in librarianship. As early as 1995, Wilder predicted that a large percentage of the ARL population would be retiring by 2020 thereby creating a vacuum of not only library leaders but also followers in academic libraries.[31] This crisis was further echoed by Martin when he found that 40 percent of librarians would be retiring by 2014.[32] Matarazzo believes that the LIS programs "do not have the capacity to replace the librarians who will be leaving the profession."[33] Consequently, not only will there be a shortage of librarians but there will also be fewer and fewer librarians who will be willing or even have the capability to step into leadership roles as the long-time leaders retire. Some libraries have begun to groom leaders within their institutions. However, this may contribute to an additional problem since, as Martin stresses, the "next generation of academic library leaders are simply a repackaging of the skills possessed by current library leaders."[34] They are not learning and developing skills for the current environment. Consequently, those groomed to be future library leaders may be taught management skills rather than leadership skills. This has created an environment where many "libraries are well managed, but many are under-led."[35]

Why is it important for libraries, particularly during this time of flux, to foster leadership throughout the library? Schreiber and Shannon believe it is important because the "hyper speed of changes in information services now demands libraries that are lean, mobile, and strategic. They must be lean to meet expanding customer expectations within the confines of limited budgets; mobile to move quickly and easily with technological and other innovations; and strategic to anticipate and plan for market changes."[36]

For libraries, the root of Schreiber and Shannon's statement revolves around increased customer expectations where today's technologically savvy users are looking for libraries to improve and implement new, faster, and innovative services to meet their needs. Libraries need leaders who can develop a strategy and then communicate it to everyone who has vested interest in the library—users, staff members, and decision-makers. The reason it is important for leaders to communicate their vision is because everyone, not just those with positional authority, must understand their library's mission so that they can anticipate and respond successfully to the user's needs.[37] If library staff, for example do not respond successfully to their user's needs and deliver what may be considered bad customer service, users will become dissatisfied with the library and will find alternatives for their information requirements and stop supporting the library altogether. This is because, in the world today, patron expectations have increased and library users believe that they should receive the same service from the library that companies such as Barnes and Noble, Amazon, and Google Scholar provide. If they don't get this personal service, they will seek an alternative source to secure their information needs.[38]

Consequently, in an attempt to remain relevant in today's fast-paced technological society, leadership needs to be spread throughout all levels of the library, and every employee must be able to foster a leadership mind-set for the whole organization. We must all examine and reexamine how the organization can remain competitive and meet the needs of their patrons. Grönfeldt and Strother stated that organizations need "to acquire a competitive advantage by placing an emphasis on a factor that is not as easy to copy as price or technology—namely, the quality of service they give to customers. Furthermore, increased competition has called attention to the growing importance of employee initiative, innovation, flexibility, and productivity as a response to pressures to adapt to external changes in the corporate environment. If organizations are to be expected to successfully plan and carry out continuous cycles of change to survive in today's service-driven economy, the exciting question of *leadership in service* arises."[39]

It is only through the examination of each individual service experience that libraries can survive. It is the end, or service experience, that informs the means, not the other way around. Although we need to give patrons what they need, we also need to consider that what they need may not necessarily be what they asked for or what they want. This responsibility is what makes service leadership different from all the other leadership theories.

The status quo in large organizations seems to be largely competitive and transactional: " . . . society has conditioned people to act in certain ways: to keep thoughts hidden, to portray oneself in the most favorable light, to create rumors or allow them to perpetuate, to use slippery language, to employ subterfuge."[40] The circumstances described are diametrically opposed to the service leadership model for a number of reasons: service leadership necessitates that there is more collaboration, less power distance and a motivation to serve. For example, many people want to be president for the authority and influence that the position gives them, and many of those individuals say that they want to serve, but much of what a candidate must do to get elected is contrary to the values of servant leadership. The concept of servant leadership is anathema to the concept of wanting to be a leader, a decision-maker, or a person in authority. It is the mission to serve that comes first, with all that entails. In some cases, those individuals may be recognized with positional authority, but in all cases, they have enormous influence on those around them. Managers or those with positional authority may or may not practice servant leadership; certainly managers have a greater opportunity to put the tenets into practice, serve others, and have a more positive impact. Managers and "leaders have a special responsibility, because the nature of their leadership puts them in a special position in which they have a greater opportunity to influence others in significant ways."[41]

Leadership is truly each of these: a trait, an ability, a skill, and a behavior. It is also a relationship between individuals and a value that can be inculcated into an organization. How the relationship is built will determine the climate in the organization and whether it is successful and sustainable.

NOTES

1. Eric Garner, *The Art of Leadership,* 46, www.stritapiret.or.id/wp-content/uploads/2013/03/the-art-of-leadership.pdf.
2. Jeanine Parolini, Kathleen Patterson, and Bruce Winston, "Distinguishing Between Transformational and Servant Leadership," *Leadership and Organization Development Journal* 30, no. 3 (2009): 274.
3. Robert K. Greenleaf, *Servant Leadership: A Journey into the Nature of Legitimate Power & Greatness* (Mahwah, NJ: Paulist, 1977), 27.

4. Mark A. Rennaker, *Listening and Persuasion: Examining the Communicative Patterns of Servant Leadership* (Regent University, 2008), 38.

5. Sen Sendjaya, James C. Sarros, and Joseph C. Santora, "Defining and Measuring Servant Leadership Behavior in Organizations," *Journal of Management Studies* 45, no. 1 (2008): 403–404.

6. Robert K Greenleaf, *The Servant Leader Within: A Transformative Path* (Mahwah, NJ: Robert K. Greenleaf Center, 2003).

7. Svafa Grönfeldt and Judith Strother, *Service Leadership: The Quest for Competitive Advantage* (Thousand Oaks, CA: Sage Publications, 2006), 24.

8. James Brian Quinn, Jordan J. Baruch, and Penny Cushman Paquette, "Technology in Service," *Scientific American* 257, no. 6 (1987): 50.

9. Leonard L. Berry, Valarie A. Zeithaml, and A. Parasuraman, "Five Imperatives for Improving Service Quality," *MIT Sloan Management Review* 31, no. 4 (1990), 29.

10. Svafa Grönfeldt and Judith Strother, *Service Leadership: The Quest for Competitive Advantage* (Thousand Oaks, CA: Sage Publications, 2006), 25.

11. Barry Bozeman, *All Organizations are Public: Comparing Public and Private Organizations* (Washington, DC: Jossey-Bass, 1987).

12. David O. Renz and Associates, *The Jossey-Bass Handbook of Nonprofit Leadership and Management,* 3rd ed. (San Francisco, CA: Wiley, 2010), 196.

13. Ibid., 195.

14. Ibid., 196.

15. Amos Lakos and Shelley Phipps, "Creating a Culture of Assessment: A Catalyst for Organizational Change," *portal: Libraries and the Academy* 4, no. 3 (2004): 350.

16. David O. Renz and Associates, *The Jossey-Bass Handbook of Nonprofit Leadership and Management,* 3rd ed. (San Francisco, CA: Wiley, 2010), 196.

17. Secretary of Defense Robert M. Gates, George Bush Award for Excellence in Public Service, 2007, www.defense.gov/Speeches/Speech.aspx?SpeechID=1190.

18. Judith B. Strother and Svafa Grönfeldt, "Service Leadership: The Challenge of Developing a New Paradigm," *2005 IEEE International Professional Communications Conference Proceedings* (2005): 65–71.

19. Ibid.

20. Ibid.

21. Jay A. Conger and Beth Benjamin, *Building Leaders: How Successful Companies Develop the Next Generation* (New York, NY: Wiley and Sons, 1999).

22. Peter Senge, "Leading Learning Organizations: The Bold, the Powerful, and the Invisible," in *The Leader of the Future*, eds. Frances Hesselbein, Marshall Goldsmith, and Richard Beckhard (San Francisco, CA: Jossey-Bass 1996), 42.

23. Peter M. Senge. "The Leader's New Work: Building Learning Organizations," *Sloan Management Review* 32, no. 1 (1990): 7.

24. Ibid.

25. Peter M. Senge. *The Fifth Discipline: The Art & Practice of the Learning Organization* (New York, NY: Doubleday, 1990), 340.

26. Ibid., 6–10.

27. Donald E. Riggs, "Crisis and Opportunities in Library Leadership," in *Library and Information Science Professions,* ed. Mark D. Winston (Binghamton, NY: Haworth Press, 2001), 7.
28. Ibid.
29. Donald Riggs, *Library Leadership: Visualizing the Future* (Phoenix, AZ: Oryx, 1982), v.
30. Donald E. Riggs, "Crisis and Opportunities in Library Leadership," in *Library and Information Science Professions,* ed. Mark D. Winston (Binghamton, NY: Haworth Press, 2001), 8.
31. Stanley J. Wilder, *The Age Demographics of Academic Librarians: A Profession Apart* (New York: NY: Routledge, 2000), 6.
32. Jason Martin, "The Art of Librarianship: Thoughts on Leadership Skills for Next Generation of Academic Library Leaders," *College & Research Libraries News* 70, no.11 (2009): 652.
33. James M. Matarazzo, "Recruitment: The Way Ahead," in *Recruiting, Education and Training Cataloging Librarians: Solving the Problems,* eds. Sheila S. Intner and Janet Swan Hill (New York, NY.: Greenwood Press, 1989), 26.
34. Jason Martin, "The Art of Librarianship: Thoughts on Leadership Skills for Next Generation of Academic Library Leaders," *College & Research Libraries News* 70, no.11 (2009): 652.
35. Donald E. Riggs, "Crisis and Opportunities in Library Leadership," in *Library and Information Science Professions,* ed. Mark D. Winston (Binghamton, NY: Haworth Press, 2001), 7.
36. Becky Schreiber and John Shannon, "Developing Library Leaders for the 21st Century," in *Leadership in the Library and Information Science Professions,* ed. Mark Winston (Binghamton, NY.: Haworth, 2001), 35–49, 36.
37. Ibid.
38. Suzanne Walters, *Customer Service: A How-To-Do It Manual for Libraries* (New York, NY: Neal-Schuman, 1994), 1.
39. Svafa Grönfeldt and Judith Strother, *Service Leadership: The Quest for Competitive Advantage* (Thousand Oaks, CA: Sage Publications, 2006), 5.
40. John Doncevic, "Servant-Leadership as a Model for Library Administration," *Catholic Library World* 73, no. 3 (2003), 173.
41. Peter G. Northouse, *Leadership: Theory and Practice* (Los Angeles, CA: SAGE Publications, 2009), 382.

CHAPTER 3

CONSCIENTIOUSNESS AS THE FOUNDATION

The best way to find yourself is to lose yourself in the service of others.
—Gandhi[1]

Conscientiousness is at the core of service leadership and has multiple meanings that are significant to it: to be guided by conscience or principles, to be careful and self-disciplined, and to be attentive to others. Conscientiousness supposes that an individual has a profound self-awareness, including their values and motivations, biases and strengths. Through this knowledge, the individual achieves a balanced perspective of themselves, their relationship with others, and their role in an organization or effort.

Conscientiousness is also defined as acting according to one's conscience. This concept is framed on a couple of assumptions; knowing oneself and acting according to personal philosophy. It is through self-reflection that one should first know what is in one's own heart and mind, assuming a certain personal morality, and that the actions of the individual as they interact with the world outside themselves align with this inner morality. This concept of conscience, in the sense of finding yourself or "knowing oneself," is pervasive in both philosophical treatises and management literature. Gandhi's statement above is a fundamental value and is emblematic of the personality and behavior of service leadership. By helping others, service leaders will be able to achieve their goals. They can only do this, though, by rising above their own individual concerns and sublimating their worries, problems, and values in favor of efforts that will benefit others. This is no easy task. In order to lose these preconceived thoughts and personal values, service leaders must be willing to go above and beyond the minimum required tasks, to be *conscientious of themselves*. The key way to do this is through *listening to oneself*. A service leader who reflects on his own ethical foundations and motivations achieves awareness of who he truly is.

In Buddhism, for example, Siddhartha Gautama, known as the first Buddha, achieved enlightenment while sitting under the Bodhi Tree in India, first in deep meditation to clear his mind of all troubles, concerns, and thoughts. Then, ultimately in mindful meditation, he allowed himself to open up to the answers to questions about *dukkha* (usually translated as suffering, this word also means change and dependence), He discovered what has become known around the world as the Middle Way, which is a path of discipline away from the extremes of self-indulgence. His self-discovery and search for inner truth led to the conception of the Eightfold Path to enlightenment, the realization that self is illusion and that dedication to serving others is fundamental to self-discovery. It is easy to see how this philosophy can be viewed as contrary to the foundation of many Western societies, which tend to view individuals or the self as unique and the basis of who we are—our core being. Throughout our lives we are brought up to believe in the core values of the society in which we live and to state that these beliefs make up our core being. But not everyone grows up in the same society. Conflicts arise because of core value disagreements. What does this mean for a service leader? Each service leader needs to listen to her core being, search for her inner truth, and recognize when she is good at something and when she is not. She needs to listen to herself and understand what her biases are toward her own beliefs and values as well as her intolerance to other beliefs and values. A service leader needs to find and understand herself before she can understand others.

CONTEMPLATION AND SELF-REFLECTION

Interestingly, listening is largely overlooked in the library literature. We may espouse listening to our patrons—and do surveys and focus groups to this end—but the literature largely ignores the disciplinary research that could inform a library's knowledge about its user groups and colleagues, particularly those in academic setting.

Before an individual can be effective at listening to others, it is critical that he first listen to himself—or pay attention to his conscience, providing the ethical foundation and the motivation that is at every individual's core. According to Spears, to be a leader one must be "in touch with one's own inner voice and seeking to understand what one's body, spirit, and mind are communicating."[2] According to servant leadership theories, listening to oneself entails two facets: contemplation and personal morality. Contemplation is the effort to "know thyself" in order to reach a "higher notion of being"[3] wherein individuals learn to harness their own potential through self-awareness. Contemplation is deliberate and thoughtful reflection without distraction. It may be contemplation of internal feelings or internal responses to the external environment but not to the point of self-absorption, or navel-gazing. This is both internal and external awareness and the willingness to see oneself honestly and without blinders or assumptions. The foundation of a service leader's self-awareness is what gives his life meaning and prompts him to act according to his personal morality. This is the moral compass or true north that is referred to by both Greenleaf and Spears, as well as in later literature on servant leadership. Leaders achieve self-awareness through being self-reflective, not self-centered, and "authentic leaders are not ego-driven, they are guided by their own true north, their own moral compasses."[4]

Before an individual can be effective at listening to others, he must first listen to himself so that he can be aware of his own personal ethics and biases. Once aware of his moral basis, he will understand his own motivation for listening.[5] Individuals who don't understand their moral basis may lose their way, becoming overwhelmed by the noise" around them and neglecting to recognize the significance of what they are listening to. On this foundation of self-awareness and self-knowledge is built a sense of morality and conviction with which leaders need to be in touch since any decision they make or action they take will be informed and directed by their ethical foundation. Service leadership prizes a universal value in that service to others; like servant leadership it nurtures the human spirit by becoming a unifying idea. In addition, the self-awareness and perception of that inner morality serve as the foundation for the commitment to serving others: "Specifying what is right and wrong, values guide and influence leader's motivational, affective, and cognitive processes and hence are important antecedents of motivation to serve."[6] In order to do this one must know what one believes. This could come at a cost because "we may resist self-knowledge to protect our self-esteem and self-respect."[7] Service leaders accept this self-awareness without ego, demonstrating that they have enough humility to not only be a keen listener who is accountable to those they serve, but also someone who sees criticism and advice as a gift in order to better serve their patrons.[8] The key for listening to oneself is self-reflection.

Self-reflection is fundamental to service leadership. No leader can become a service leader if their mental model, or the way in which they perceive the world, is not achieved through self-reflection. Mental models are the outward application of inner development. In other words, "there is a close connection between our sense of self and the feelings we have about others."[9] The constant learning and development require self-reflection and self-honesty; to know how to improve or evolve, it is necessary to know where there is deficiency or where a mistake was made. ". . . the brain soaks up life's lessons to better prepare us for the next time we face a similar challenge, uncertainty, or decision point."[10] Senge discusses self-reflection and change with regard to personal mastery, which is composed of "continually clarifying what is important to us . . . [and] . . . continually learning how to see the current reality more clearly."[11] One definitely influences the other. He defines personal mastery as "the discipline of continually clarifying and deepening our personal vision of focusing our energies, of developing patience, and of seeing reality objectively."[12]

In the vignette on Service Leadership in Practice, Rose is not a leader with positional authority, but she holds the values that employees consider important

SERVICE LEADERSHIP IN PRACTICE

Rose is asked by her library director to take over the responsibilities of head of collection development. Rose is hesitant to accept the position, concerned about her lack of supervisory experience. Aware of her own limitations, Rose asks the library director to give her a few days to think over this opportunity. That evening, Rose goes home and begins to reflect on her job performance as well as her feelings about where the library profession is going and her ability to lead in that direction. Although extremely intelligent and good at her job, Rose recognizes that she is proud of being an "old school" librarian who has continually questioned whether technology should drive service and developments in the library. "Why," she questioned herself, "why do I do that? Is it because I believe that technology will obliterate the profession as I know it or is it because I am uncomfortable with change?" Being honest with herself, she was surprised to admit to herself that she was uncomfortable with change and if she took this position, not only would she have to embrace change but she would also have to lead it. The next day, Rose met with the library director to let her know that she did not believe she was the best person for the job. When Rose acknowledged her biases and limitations, she was acting in the best interest of the library—not her own—showing that she had enough respect for the library director to be honest about her own shortcomings.

for a leader to have. Employees believe that their leader needs to act according to the values that make up their core moral foundation. If a leader does indeed exhibit and model these values, employees will then confirm their own behavior in the behavior demonstrated by their leader. According to Russell, an effective leader's moral foundation encompasses integrity that results from four essential values:

1. Truth-telling;
2. Promise-keeping;
3. Fairness; and
4. Respect for the individual.[13]

Rose demonstrates self-awareness because her moral foundation not only encompasses the values important to other employees within the organization but she also demonstrates these values even when it would be at a financial disadvantage for her to do so. By acting according to her values and standing firm in her beliefs, Rose created trust and increased her credibility with other employees in the organization in her beliefs.

Awareness

Olson states that a "leader seeks out the why behind the words and actions of others and themselves, those words and actions that don't appear to build each other up. The leader knows that a person's perception or paradigm is his reality. Yet a servant leader goes beyond that perception or paradigm and seeks to understand the other person."[14] So the question we must ask is, "What motivates a service leader to do something or act in a specific way?" The first step of self-discovery is awareness. However, as Spears indicates, "Making a commitment to foster awareness can be scary—you never know what you may discover."[15] This is particularly true when what you discover is something about yourself that goes against long-held beliefs or values.

Consider the story of Rose, above. Although great at her job, Rose was resistant to change, particularly technological change. She worried that she, personally, and the profession, more globally, might be replaced by technology. This self-awareness humbled her and made her aware of her own limitations. Greenleaf stated that "Awareness is not a giver of solace—it is just the opposite. It is a disturber and an awakener. Able leaders are usually sharply awake and reasonably disturbed. They are not seekers after solace. They have their own inner serenity."[16] This is why in our example above, Rose turned down the position. She was aware that the position would call for her to lead change, and she decided that she was not able to commit to this. This is why "there is no substitute for fashioning your own framework, your own operating philosophy. This philosophy—which reflects one's core beliefs and view of people, society, and the world—provides the intellectual and moral foundation for an agenda."[17] Service leadership is committed to empowering and promoting integrity in others, addressing both being true to oneself and helping others to reach their full potential. True self-examination leads to recognition of one's shortcomings and opportunities for development. In this way, acknowledging weakness makes one stronger, not only because it allows one to strive to ameliorate any weaknesses but it also demonstrates integrity and self-confidence. By taking responsibility for mistakes, an individual signals a willingness to learn and improve. "Gaining self-knowledge, therefore, requires that we accept what we learn as neutral information, neither positive nor negative, that will enhance the strong capabilities that we already possess."[18]

Admitting mistakes and weaknesses has several positive outcomes:

- It humanizes and thus may build sympathy;
- It models behavior for others—that it is okay to take responsibility for mistakes;

- By taking responsibility, the problem can be addressed;
- Through acknowledgment of a problem, there is the commitment to learn and improve; without this acknowledgement, the problem does not get resolved, often causing more issues.

This self-awareness sets the stage for interacting with others and within the organization in a positive and effective manner. Before engaging with others, a service leader must not only examine her own perspective and how it may impact her perception of a situation, but she must also deal with the situation effectively.

Consideration and Inspiration

Conscientiousness also recalls the fundamental belief in moral leadership that is the foundation of Burns' transformational leadership theory. The morality that is referred to here is not related to a specific religion; it refers instead to a universal concept on which many religions are based that has its roots in Greek philosophy, similar to the Golden Rule or to the concept of Do unto others as you would have them do unto you. This self-awareness and introspection is core: ". . . the essential quality that sets servant-leaders apart from others is that they live by their conscience—the inward moral sense of what is right and what is wrong . . . Conscience is the moral law within. It is the overlapping of moral law and behavior."[19]

Conscientiousness is an altruistic philosophy based in the concept of service, "leaders demonstrate an altruistic mindset."[20] It is not the intent to lead that is uppermost in a leader's mind, but the intent to serve that prompts him to exhibit inspirational behavior that others would follow.

While it seems simple, conscientiousness actually encompasses some intricate constructs. First, it assumes an ethical foundation or personal morality. Second, it entails individual reflection or contemplation of this code. And finally, it has implications for an individual's own mind, perceptions, morals, and behavior.

The courage to speak up shifts focus externally so that one is more present to serve others. This may appear as advocating on behalf of individuals, but it is more of a consequence of the primary motivation to work toward the moral end, to do what is right. To be present "is not just being here or being there, but having your whole self-available at all times—available to yourself as you try to bring all your values to bear on the work at hand, and available to others as you respond to the problems and issues and challenges of team members, colleagues, managers, employees, vendors, and customers."[21] Sendjaya states that "servant leadership shares similar key characteristics with authentic leadership, in that both explicitly recognize the importance of positive moral perspective, self-awareness, self-regulation (i.e., authentic behavior), positive modeling, and a focus on follower development . . ."[22] Servant leaders exhibit a philanthropic outlook and are dedicated to those they serve. However, far too often we view our leaders as being uncooperative, micromanaging, self-absorbed, and authoritarian. These types of Machiavellian leaders "stand in a stark contrast to a servant leader. In a typical leader-follower relationship, the former subscribes to the view that 'the end justifies the means,' whereas the latter believes that both the ends and means should be morally justifiable."[23] It is disheartening to hear authors such as Russell state that we are experiencing a leadership crisis because self-interest motivates many leaders.[24]

This assumes that there are very few leaders who are altruistic and motivated to help others even at the risk or sacrifice to themselves—that service leaders are rare, even in service organizations. Service leaders are defined as individuals who "do the right thing—even when inconvenient or expensive. They place a premium on being fair, consistent, and truthful with customers, employees, suppliers, and other stakeholders, thereby earning the opportunity to lead."[25]

Honesty and Integrity

A large part of trust rests with a service leader's ability to be honest with herself and others. Built on this foundation of self-awareness and knowing oneself is a sense of morality and conviction, what is ultimately right and just and how to act with integrity and compassion. Northouse asserts that "ethics has to do with what leaders do and who leaders are" and goes on to say that "in any decision-making situation, ethical issues are either implicitly or explicitly involved. The choices leaders make and how they respond in a given situation are informed and directed by their ethics."[26] Being honest to yourself and others is important.

Integrity refers to the individual's internal life and personality, as well as his dialogue with and perception of the external world and its influences. The foundation of effective leadership is integrity, in the sense of being whole as well as being true to oneself in both thought and action. This necessitates that an individual be honest with himself about his strengths and weaknesses, transparent about his motivations and values, and that he align word and deed with his belief. This self-awareness or self-knowledge comes through reflection and thoughtfulness.

Integrity of this is the understanding of an individual's place in the world, not just in terms of worth but in terms of how their smallest action (or inaction) can impact the larger world. It requires an attention to both the forest and the trees—the big picture balanced with individual and incremental actions. It is not uncommon for an individual, particularly a leader, to compromise individual concerns, either his own or those of other people in the organization, for the greater good. This Machiavellian approach assumes that the leader is the individual who defines the greater good for the organization and that his perspective is not impaired. In some organizations administrators may define the organization as a reflection of themselves, not dissimilar from the way that a monarch imposes his own self-interest on his country through use of the royal *we*, sometimes to its detriment. This kind of self-deception is a notable example; it is much more commonplace to see it in an organization, both from managers and from employees who do not have positional authority.

The issue of compromise is also one of fundamental concern. In some cases it is viewed as a skill, like diplomacy, and that win-win solutions are the ideal. However, compromise in this instance can also describe the undermining of an individual's ethical core for the greater good. When this occurs an individual is not a leader but an administrator because a leader will strive to be true to his or her principles. This may be indicated by the fact a true service leader will place service and empowerment above the desire for power and authority. It may be argued that this is why it is unusual for a service leader to be successful in public office or even to seek out highly political administrative positions.

The implications of this concept can be easily transferred to individuals in a service organization such as a library and are greater than just the impact on one individual. Burley-Allen defines a model for how a single situation evolves and can impact the performance not just of the individual but of the larger organization:

- situation;
- thought process;
- behavior; and
- feeling.[27]

Individuals may experience a situation or event and respond to it differently, but as they interact and communicate (either verbally or through behavior), they may influence each other, the organization, and the organization's climate.

Authenticity and Trust

There is so much in the literature on leadership that investigates specific traits, characteristics, or behaviors of effective leaders. There are multitudes of research studies, articles in trade journals, and popular books that advise individuals about how to act like a leader. It is impossible to know what the inner discourse is for any individual other than ourselves. Treatises and workshops that teach how to act like a leader are superficial and many individuals treat becoming a leader like putting on a new suit of clothes: the image looks good but there is nothing on the inside. In other words, it lacks sincerity or integrity. Leadership, particularly servant leadership, is not about the image someone projects or the words they use—it is about what they do and how their actions are reflections of their integrity. Personal integrity "enable[s] them to act with the conviction and authenticity that resonance requires."[28]

This is not to say that such studies are not of benefit, but the transformational change is internal, not external, and evidenced only by their actions and interactions. Covey discusses the necessity of working from the inside–out, which "means to start first with self—to start with the most inside part of self—with your paradigms, your character, and your motives"[29] and that by striving for personal greatness and modeling values, there will be more successful outcomes externally. Being a model of those personal and organizational values, suiting action to words, also addresses inspirational motivation. In order to gain the trust of employees (or anyone), you must be worthy of it. Service leaders understand that their word is their bond and that when they lose the trust of those for whom and with whom they work, they also lose the ability to inspire and motivate those around them and to be effective in the organization. They may lose this trust by not being true to their values, losing track of who they are, and no longer listening to the inner voice reminding them of what they believe in and stand for. They may become secretive and no longer model transparency throughout the organization. They project an image of a person who says one thing but does another.

Transparency and modeling are related: transparency is permitting the inner values to be revealed; modeling is connecting action to belief. This addresses the outward presentation of the self and how one interacts with the world. Modeling one's own values may lead to an individual becoming a role model and thus may promote integrity and transparency in others and in the organization. Sendjaya supports positive modeling to "encourage followers to demonstrate consistency between what they say and do, transparency about their limitations, and engagement in moral reasoning."[30]

Service leadership accepts that trust is critical to any relationship, whether it be a relationship with family, friends, employees, colleagues, or clients. The way service leaders gain trust is by being true to themselves and the values they hold dear. People are inspired by a leader who acts according to their values, and when leaders act contrary to their values they lose trust. Imagine if you will a leader who continually says to her team that empowerment is important not only for employees but for library patrons; in the same day she does a 180-degree turn and doesn't empower a library patron with the information and knowledge to make an informed decision. It is hard to trust someone who says one thing but does the opposite. If a leader continues to exhibit negative behaviors such as: conceit, untrustworthiness, and insensitivity, she will lose credibility. These types of negative behaviors corrode the components of an honest relationship. Employees who see their leader say one thing and to do another realize that they cannot rely on their boss to do what she said she would do. However, telling the truth is a two-way street. Not only do employees want to hear the truth, but they must also feel comfortable to tell the truth to their boss. Service leaders realize that without trust it is impossible to implement and sustain change within an. After all, "if we weren't willing to tell a client the kind truth, why should they pay us?"[31]

Values and Decision-Making

Once a service leader becomes aware of her own values and biases, she can use this information to assess the situation when making decisions.

In the Service Leadership in Practice box below, Jillian needed to be aware of her biases before she could make an ethical decision about the e-book vendor. She avoided a conflict of interest issue because she first assessed the current situation by communicating with others to identify the library's real needs over her own self-interest. Service leadership acknowledges that "no single value or set of values is always accepted as universal,"[32] and as a result not everyone is going to agree with each other's ethical value system, particularly if these values affect the way they make decisions. This is why professional ethics were created to ensure that despite the differences in individual values a professional values system would be followed. However, if a person does not follow the ethical standards of the profes-

SERVICE LEADERSHIP IN PRACTICE

Jillian, the head of acquisition at a large academic library, began the process of evaluating vendors' responses to a request for proposals to be the library's e-book vendor. Before she begins to assess the information, Jillian builds a metric of what the library needs in an e-book vendor. As she begins to fill out the metrics, Jillian places a number of questionable important needs, such as content, on the list. Jillian begins to question her own biases. Why is science coverage for e-books more important than humanities coverage, particularly when the university for which Jillian works is known for its strong humanities curriculum? Jillian soon realizes that she has bias toward science over humanities because she studied biology. Coming to this recognition, Jillian speaks to other collection development librarians to see what they feel is more important, science or humanities. Jillian is surprised to discover that a strong humanities collection was indeed what the university needed in an e-book vendor, not a strong science collection. As a result, Jillian changed the metrics.

sion, then both the standards and the profession are at risk of deteriorating and eventually betraying the trust of those they serve. According to vanDuinkerken et al, "The reason for this risk of failure rests on how people judge the actions and behaviors of both the individual librarians and the librarian profession itself. If the profession fails to develop and maintain its ethical standards, the librarianship professions will fail because society will lose confidence in the profession."[33] Hence it is necessary that any profession, including the library profession create and cultivate external standards such as a code of ethics so that the profession can generate a reputation for dependability, integrity, and proficiency.[34]

ETHICAL LEADERSHIP: ALTRUISM AND COMMITMENT TO SERVICE

Ethical leadership plays a huge part in leadership and service. It is "rooted in respect, service, justice, honesty, and community"[35] and may be exemplified in one of three fundamental philosophies:

1. Ethical egoism: states that individuals will act in their own best interest: "self-interest is an ethical stance closely related to transactional leadership theories."[36]
2. Utilitarianism: advocates "the greatest good for the greatest number."[37]
3. Altruism: "suggests that actions are moral if their primary purpose is to promote the best interests of others," and it is the basis for transformational leadership.[38]

Altruistic behavior rests at the core of the service model: ". . . leaders are truly effective only when they are motivated by a concern for others, when their actions are guided primarily by the criteria of 'the benefit to others even if it results in some cost to self.'"[39] In the sidebar above, Rose turned down her promotion at a cost to herself but to the benefit of others. If she accepted the position, she would have struggled to achieve what the library needed her to do. However, not only did she remain true to her ethical beliefs, she also recognized that she would not be able to meet the needs of the people she would be leading.

Authenticity and transparency, which will be discussed later, help build credibility and trust. As stated above, understanding of oneself comes from self-reflection and ultimately promotes understanding of others and the external world. "As we practice self-discovery and reflection, we become more adept at decoding the feelings of others."[40] This comprehension breeds understanding and patience: ". . . humility is the mother of all other virtues—because it promotes stewardship"[41] and service. Self-knowledge also breeds confidence. "While to be authentic is to be honest, to be vulnerable is openness about that honesty. In practice it means to question a plan or idea—especially when everyone else seems to agree without critical analysis. This is especially important in libraries where the prevalent method to obtain ideas is by committee . . . It means to hold a view when that is the most reasonable or just one—especially when the majority of people believe otherwise."[42]

While ethics are exemplified by individual action, they can also be defined by a community, organization or even as a profession. This shared standard of ethical conduct informs the individual and their behavior.

PROFESSIONAL STANDARDS: ALA CODE OF ETHICS

Service librarianship is defined by the American Library Association Code of Ethics. On March 30, 1930, the ALA Committee on Ethics released its Suggested Code of Ethics in the *Bulletin of the American Library Association*. This code laid out the ethical principles associated with the structure, governance, and operation of a library, but it lacked ethical guidance for those day-to-day ethical issues that librarians face. In 1939 the code was revised and shifted its previous structure and focus to concentrate on what librarians do day to day. This was accomplished by establishing a code of ethics with 28 standards of ethical conduct for the relationship between the following:

- librarians and the library administration;
- librarians and their colleagues; and
- librarians and the library community.

Over time additional ethical standards where developed to reflect the librarian's changing professional values. These values were articulated in the establishment of ALA's *Library Bill of Rights Statement* of 1948 (revisions 1961, 1967, and 1980) and its *Freedom to Read Statement* (1953), which would later act as the catalyst for future revisions of the ALA *Code of Ethics* in 1981, 1995, and 2008.

Despite the creation and continual development of ethical codes, service leaders are aware that individual values and the values of the professional codes that they support can be contrary to the policies of the institutions where they work. Take for example academic institutions that charge their students a fee for library services. This fee may be difficult for librarians to agree with since they have supported a code that calls for free information to all. It is where pragmatism meet ideals—and it usually requires compromising one if not both. Librarians will continue to face many ethical conflicts when their own beliefs differ from library policies and their professional ethical codes.

REFLECTIONS ON CONSCIENTIOUSNESS: TOOLS FOR DEVELOPMENT

1. Align behavior with belief. Ask yourself, as you go through your day, do your actions reflect your inner beliefs or thoughts? Does the inner dialogue correlate with the external dialogue and action? If not, why?
2. Find your triggers. What are the topics, situations, or individuals that prompt you to stop listening? When do they occur and what are they?
3. Lies that we tell ourselves. Is there feedback or information that you have been given that completely contradicts your own perception? How is it counter to your own self concept? How would you go about gaining an objective perspective?
4. Know your strengths and weaknesses. Kouzes and Posner advise several steps for clarifying personal values, among them to "look in the mirror, take time for contemplation . . . write your credo . . . audit your ability to succeed."[43]
5. The true measure of someone's character is how they react in a crisis. When you are stressed or in a situation that could be considered an emergency, how do you act? How do you treat others?
6. Don't know something once a day. Particularly in libraries in which information is a commodity, acknowledge an area of ignorance and actively seek out an opportunity to learn something from someone else.

NOTES

1. "12 Great Quotes from Gandhi on His Birthday," *Forbes,* October 2, 2012, www.forbes.com/sites/ashoka/2012/10/02/12-great-quotes-from-gandhi-on-his-birthday.
2. Larry C. Spears, "Tracing the Past, Present, and Future of Servant-Leadership," in *Focus on Leadership: Servant-Leadership for the Twenty-First Century,* eds. Larry C. Spears and Michele Lawrence (New York: NY: Greenleaf Center for Servant-Leadership, 2002), 5.
3. Don M. Frick, *Robert K. Greenleaf: A Life of Servant Leadership* (San Francisco, CA: Berrett-Koehler, 2004), xvii.
4. Filippa Marullo Anzalone "Servant Leadership: A New Model for Law Library Leaders," *Law Library Journal* 99, no. 4 (2007): 804.
5. James W. Sipe and Don M. Frick, *Seven Pillars of Servant Leadership: Practicing the Wisdom of Leading by Serving* (Mahwah, NJ: Paulist Press, 2009), 58.
6. Kok-Yee Ng and Christine S. K. Koh, "Motivation to Serve: Understanding the Heart of the Servant-Leader and Servant Leadership Behaviors," in *Servant Leadership: Developments in Theory,* eds. Dirk van Dierendonck and Kathleen Patterson (New York: Macmillan, 2010): 96.
7. Lao Tzu and Tao Te Ching, "Listening to Ourselves," in *Listening to Conflict: Finding*

Constructive Solutions to Workplace Disputes, ed. Erik J. Van Slyke (New York, NY: American Management Association, 1999), 34.

8. Kathleen Ann Patterson, "Servant Leadership: A Theoretical Model" (dissertation, Regent University 2003), 15.

9. Erich Fromm, "Selfishness and Self-Love," *Psychiatry, Journal for the Study of Interpersonal Process,* 2 (1939): 507–523.

10. Goleman, R. Boyatzis and A. McKee, *Primal Leadership: Realizing the Power of Emotional Intelligence* (Boston, MA: Harvard Business School Press, 2002), 44.

11. Peter M. Senge, *The Fifth Discipline: The Art & Practice of the Learning Organization* (New York, NY: Doubleday, 1990), 141.

12. Ibid., 7.

13. Robert F. Russell and A. Gregory Stone, "A Review of Servant Leadership Attributes: Developing a Practice Model," *Leadership and Organization Development Journal* 23 no. 3 (2002): 148.

14. Nancy J. Olson, "Refreshing Your Philosophy of Servant Leadership as a Christian Librarian," *Christian Librarian* 53, no. 2 (2010): 50.

15. Larry C. Spears, "The Understanding and Practice of Servant-Leadership," in *Practicing Servant Leadership: Succeeding through Trust, Bravery, and Forgiveness,* ed. L. C. Spears and M. Lawrence (San Francisco, CA : Jossey-Bass, 2004), 13.

16. Robert K. Greenleaf, *The Power of Servant-Leadership*, ed. Larry C. Spears (San Francisco, CA: Berrett-Koehler, 1998), 6.

17. Richard N. Haass, *The Bureaucratic Entrepreneur: How to be Effective in Any Unruly Organization* (Washington, DC: Brookings Institution, 1999): 31.

18. Lao Tzu and Tao Te Ching, "Listening to Ourselves," in *Listening to Conflict: Finding Constructive Solutions to Workplace Disputes,* ed. Erik J. Van Slyke (New York, NY: American Management Association, 1999), 34.

19. Robert K. Greenleaf, *The Power of Servant-Leadership,* ed. Larry C. Spears (San Francisco, CA: Berrett-Koehler, 1998), 4.

20. Curtis D. Beck, "Antecedents of Servant Leadership: A Mixed Methods Study" (dissertation, University of Nebraska at Lincoln, 2010), 67.

21. James A. Autry, *The Servant Leader: How to Build a Creative Team, Develop Great Morale, and Improve Bottom-Line Performance* (New York: Prima, 2001), 18.

22. Sen Sendjaya, James C. Sarros, and Joseph C. Santora, "Defining and Measuring Servant Leadership Behavior in Organizations," *Journal of Management Studies* 45, no. 1 (2008): 403–404.

23. Sen Sendjaya and Brian Cooper, "Servant Leadership Behaviour Scale: A Hierarchical Model and Test of Construct Validity," *European Journal of Work and Organizational Psychology* 20, no. 3 (2011): 421.

24. Robert Russell, "The Role of Values in Servant Leadership," *Journal Leadership and Organization Development* 22, no. 2 (2000): 76.

25. Leonard L. Berry, *On Great Service: A Framework for Action* (New York, NY: Free Press, 1995), 15.

26. Peter G. Northouse, *Leadership: Theory and Practice* (Los Angeles, CA: SAGE Publications, 2009), 378.

27. Madelyn Burley-Allen, *Listening the Forgotten Skill: A Self-Teaching Guide,* 2nd ed. (New York: John Wiley, 1995), 85.

28. Goleman, R. Boyatzis and A. McKee. *Primal Leadership: Realizing the Power of Emotional Intelligence.* (Boston, MA: Harvard Business School Press, 2002), 40.

29. Steven R. Covey, *Principle-Centered Leadership,* (New York, NY: Simon & Schuster, 1992), 63.

30. Sen Sendjaya, James C. Sarros, and Joseph C. Santora, "Defining and Measuring Servant Leadership Behavior in Organizations," *Journal of Management Studies* 45, no. 1 (2008): 404.

31. Patrick M. Lencioni, *Getting Naked: A Business Fable about Shedding the Three Fears That Sabotage Client Loyalty* (San Francisco: CA: John Wiley & Sons, 2009), 78.

32. Matthew W. Seeger, *Ethics and Organizational Communication* (Cresskill, NJ. Hampton Press, 1997), 3.

33. Wyoma vanDuinkerken, Wendi Arant Kaspar, and Jeanne Harrell, *Guide to Ethics in Acquisitions* (New York: Scarecrow Press, Inc., 2014), forthcoming.

34. Ibid.

35. Peter G. Northouse, *Leadership: Theory and Practice* (Los Angeles, CA: SAGE Publications, 2009), 404.

36. Ibid., 379.

37. Ibid., 379.

38. Ibid., 380.

39. Rabindra Kanungo and Manuel Mendonca, *Ethical Dimensions of Leadership* (Thousand Oaks, CA: Sage Publications, 1996), 35.

40. Filippa Marullo Anzalone, "Servant Leadership: *A New Model for Law Library Leaders,*" *Law Library Journal* 99, no. 4 (2007): 800.

41. Steven R. Covey, *Principle-Centered Leadership* (New York, NY: Simon & Schuster, 1992), 54.

42. John Doncevic, "Servant-Leadership as a Model for Library Administration," *Catholic Library World* 73, no. 3 (2003): 175.

43. James M. Kouzes and Barry Z. Posner, *The Leadership Challenge,* 3rd ed. (San Francisco, CA: Jossey-Bass, 2002), 73.

CHAPTER 4

....

BUILDING RAPPORT

....

Lord, grant that I may not seek so much to be understood as to understand.
—*Saint Francis*[1]

S ervice leadership is exemplified by the consideration of others and their needs; the most fundamental expression of this value is through listening to others, demonstrating that what they have to communicate is worth the time and attention. It expresses that the speaker is valued, which strengthens not just the communication between them but also the relationship. This chapter will focus on the importance that service leaders give to listening to others as a way of building rapport, not only among their individual team members but also among all library staff members and patrons. Service leaders model open conversation and communication of concern for people while encouraging diverse opinions. Because listening is so foundational to service leadership, this chapter will highlight listening tools to build rapport.

LISTENING TO OTHERS

Hearing someone speak is not the same as listening to and understanding what they are saying. Bell and Smith define hearing as "the physical capacity to sense sounds,"[2] but that is not the same thing as listening. Take, for example, the sounds that a newborn baby makes. A person can hear these sounds but not understand what the baby is trying to communicate; therefore, the person is not really listening to what the child is saying. Conversely, the baby can hear its parents but will not understand the meaning of their words. This is why "the perception of meaning and the sometimes difficult task of achieving understanding both require the power to listen."[3] If the adult wants to stop the baby from crying, then he or she needs to understand what the baby is trying to communicate.

Listening, more broadly thought of as communication, is widely recognized as crucial to any organization if the number of management books and articles, professional development workshops, and overall attention given to the topic are any indication of its importance. In the literature and in practice, more consideration seems to be given to the transmitting aspect of communication: talking, presenting, and communicating one's message. This is particularly accurate when looking at development for managers, where the underlying assumption is often that communication is unidirectional and that the person in authority should be listened to. This attitude may be expressed by managers when addressing their efforts to improve communication in this way, "I (the manager) will communicate my message more clearly and you (the employee) will need to listen more closely."

Although talking is often considered the primary mode of communication, listening is arguably the most fundamental of the behaviors in any kind of successful leadership or management role, and, indeed, in the practice of service

SERVICE LEADERSHIP IN PRACTICE

Sara, a reference librarian, was chosen by the head of reference to plan and implement a new virtual reference system. The funding had been identified and awarded through a grant, but the functionality and the system had not been chosen. Sara's responsibility was to coordinate the effort and get buy-in from those who would be using the system—and ultimately to make it happen. Knowing this was a new service that had the possibility of reaching many more patrons, she understood that its success really rested on the engagement of those who would be providing the service. She wondered how best to get their input and their buy-in.

For many similar initiatives in the library, the outreach was just sending out an e-mail asking for feedback. But often there was little response back to those making suggestions and they ultimately felt left out of the loop and unheard. Sara had experienced this herself and knew that it could doom an organizational effort to failure either because important details or concerns were ignored or because those who were charged with actually executing the service were not invested in it.

The turnaround time for this project was short, but Sara made the time to host a forum for anyone interested. This generated a lot of interest from people who would help provide the service as well as others in the library whom Sara had not anticipated would care. One of the outcomes of the forum, generated by the group, was the formation of taskforces focusing on different aspects of functionality, implementation, and training. The systems were evaluated, one was chosen and configured, standards and policies were developed, and a training plan created and executed—on schedule and with full support of all the staff involved.

leadership. This may be the reason why DeGraaf, Tilley, and Neal are not alone when they recognized listening as the foundation upon which many other leadership behaviors are built.[4] This critical skill is given a great deal of consideration because listening is one of the most important ways in which leaders can meet the needs of others and acknowledge that people are valued and respected, which benefits an organization in a number of ways.[5] The most significant, but by no means the only, benefit is the gathering of information, or in a more strategic sense, intelligence, in order to make an educated decision. Without the correct information, individuals will be unsuccessful in understanding the situation and, consequently, be unable to make decisions that will address it effectively.

Listening enhances communication and transfer of information, which successful leaders in any organization must be able to do to make effective decisions. Ineffective decisions may be indicated within organizations by unsuccessful projects, waste of resources, and general organizational dysfunction. The successes of an organization and an individual's success within the organization will depend on making good decisions. However, the only way to make effective decisions is to be aware of all the information that affects or could affect that situation. This information can come from many different sources and in many different forms of communication, but perhaps the most important is verbal communication from stakeholders within the organization as well as outside. A leader can only be successful in making those decisions if they are truly listening to what is being said and what is not being said and if individuals feel that the service leader is approachable.

By listening to others, a service leader is effective and "can move organizations from current to future states, create visions of potential opportunities for organizations, instill within employees commitment to change, and instill new cultures and strategies in organizations that mobilize and focus energy and resources."[6] However, to achieve these outcomes, the efforts that transmit these essential leadership characteristics, such as a vision, must be effectively communicated. Consequently, listening to others in order to understand context is a key factor in achieving a service leadership model within an organization. Through the act of listening selflessly and being aware of others, a service leader can build a stronger and more effective relationship with the speaker. Listening will have the most profound impact on building a relationship with others, whether they are employees, patrons, or colleagues: "It [listening] builds our self-esteem, shows we have worth, informs us that we are not alone, helps us work through our problems, causes us to feel important and respected as a person, and tells us the other person is interested in me. We all need these things, which is why listening is such an important skill to develop and nurture."[7] Listening also advances interpersonal communication and sustains the organization and its culture in the following ways:

- It will "identify the will of a group and helps clarify that will."[8]
- It will "demonstrate respect and appreciation of others."[9]
- It will enhance communication clarity.[10]
- It will focus attention on the speaker.
- It will help lead to leader-follower trust.[11]
- It will motivate and build strength in others.

Despite the advantages listed above and the fact that managers or those with positional authority spend 80 percent of their day engaged in communication—approximately 60 percent of which is spent listening—it is alarming that individuals are only about 25 percent effective as active listeners.[12] The reason for this, Burley-Allen believes, is that people tend to assume that effective listening is the equivalent of hearing, which is a relatively passive exercise in a physical sense.[13] This mistaken assumption may lead people to believe that effective listening is internal, and consequently they may make little if any effort to study or improve their listening skills. As a result they may neglect a vital communication skill and overlook an opportunity for educational development, the potential for improved self-reflection, and the capacity to be receptive to acknowledging and correcting miscommunications and mistakes.

In libraries, as well as in other service organizations, individuals listen closely to their patrons and strive to provide them what they need. This same motivation and method of listening to patrons—listening with respect, regardless of who the speaker is and what role they play—should also be applied to employees and colleagues:. This is fundamental because the commitment to service is not based on who is being helped but is a fundamental value of service leadership. Modeling this value says something about the integrity and sincerity of the servant leader rather than how they differentiate relationships based on role. It is similar to an individual aligning his actions with his words; in this case, they simply treat everyone with empathy and strive to be of service to everyone, in whatever form that help takes for whatever role the individual has.

Depending on the situation, Burley-Allen believes that listening to others occurs on three different levels:

1. empathetic listening;
2. hearing words but not really listening; and
3. listening in spurts.[14]

Empathetic listening is presented as the highest level of listening, the goal in almost every interaction. Unlike the listener who is hearing the words, but not really listening, the empathetic listener focuses on the words and nonverbal cues in order to understand the meaning of the words as well as the speaker's intent. Empathetic listeners focus on the speaker and refrain from forming any sort of judgment about what the speaker is saying. Unlike the listener who is hearing the words, but not really listening, the empathetic listener does not stay separate from the exchange but rather concentrates on building a connection with the speaker, focusing on what is being said and on the feeling of how it is being said. The empathetic listener places himself in the other's position, attempting to see things from the speaker's point of view—the opposite of what a listener who listens in spurts does.

People who listen in spurts are passive listeners and focus on themselves rather than the speaker. They do not listen to the speaker in order to understand the whole problem, but rather so they can try to predict what the speaker will say and frame their own response. Empathetic listeners, on the other hand, do not let themselves become distracted by attempts to predict what the speaker will say next but remain aware throughout the whole listening process of what is actually being said, making the effort to listen for meaning. In order to accomplish this goal, the empathetic listener will show the speaker with both verbal and nonverbal cues that he or she is truly listening. Empathetic listeners therefore acknowledge and respond to the speaker while fully attending to the speaker's complete message "including body language, being empathic to the speaker's feelings and thoughts, and suspending one's own thoughts and feeling[s] to give attention solely to listening."[15]

Listening to others encompasses several facets: verbal, nonverbal, and a person's actions. Most communication in the workplace focuses on verbal interaction and, ideally, on effective speaking and active listening. However, what is not said, such as deliberately ignoring an issue, is as significant as what is said. This may also be what people refer to as the elephant in the room, when the silence is screaming: "It can be so cold that you shudder in response to it; it can be so warm that you are encouraged to continue and feel supported by it; or it can be a neutral message to continue talking."[16] That said many studies show that nonverbal cues (gestures, eye contact, etc.) may account for as much as 70 percent of the message, a detail that may be intuitively understood but which is given little attention outside professional development seminars and the communication literature. This is why service leaders pay so much attention to nonverbal communication.

Perhaps the most significant nonverbal cue is action: "Actions speak louder than words" and "walk the talk" are familiar phrases descriptive of someone whose words and actions are consistent. People know that they can believe what an individual says, and that she will follow through, because this individual's historic actions support what she says; in other words, she models what she says and does what she advocates.

SERVICE LEADERSHIP IN PRACTICE

Think back to a time when you had a leader who was saying one thing but his body language was saying something else. For example, your department leader Jim says he supports the CEO's decision to relocate the company that you have been working at for more than 10 years to a larger city 200 miles away because of better business connections or opportunities. You have always been aware that Jim does not like large cities because of the traffic congestion and long commutes. As Jim announces this to your department, his words are supportive but you can tell by his clenched fists, firm stance, and flippant comments that he does not support the move. Jim could either be unaware of his own biases, coming across as being non-supportive of the company's relocation, or he could be intentionally communicating his displeasure in a passive-aggressive or sarcastic manner. Regardless of whether Jim's behavior is intentional or not, his words do not correspond with his actions.

OPEN CONVERSATION AND MORAL DIALOGUE

Listening, as stated above, is not as easy as it sounds and seems to be an art that few leaders have mastered. This is why it is important for service leaders to encourage open conversation and moral dialogue among their team members with the focus on listening to what others are saying. Why then, if listening is so critical to the effective operation and success of an organization, is poor listening so common in the organizations of today? The reason most managers struggle with listening may rest in the type of personalities they possess or in the role that they are given in the organization and how individuals react to that role. Leaders, whether through the authority that a leadership position extends or through their own influence, are assertive and, as such, tend to speak up and give voice to their concerns or perspectives. Because they communicate with integrity and honesty, it may be intimidating to others. They often convey confidence and personal conviction that may be perceived as arrogance or an unwillingness to listen. While image is NOT reality, it can have a negative impact on communication and close down the conversation.

Overassertive leaders can fall into a trap of being so focused on the goal or getting results that they neglect to get buy-in and input from others and may become annoyed and dismissive with those who want to slow down the process in order to investigate possible issues. The overassertive leader may perceive those who question as resisters to change, disorganized employees, unproductive performers who only want to push their own personal agenda, and detractors of the overall organization. Consequently, when a leader hears the employee raise concerns, he may become dismissive, responding with "I hear what you are saying but . . ." Even worse, after the meeting is over the leader may talk about the person negatively with other members of the organization. When this happens, not only is the leader being unprofessional, but the leader has not heard the person and has actually rejected the employee's point of view. Instead, the leader should reflect back on what the employee said, saying "this is what I hear you saying," which is an opening for more dialogue.

Greenleaf defined listening as "an attitude toward other people and what they are attempting to express."[17] For a service leader this is the basis for participating in a conversation. True listening occurs when one stands back and listens with reverence, thoughtfulness, and empathy without judging what the other person is saying. In this way, a service leader can meet the needs of the speaker so that they can both achieve their goals. Service leaders not only focus on the other person in order to be persistently attentive to their needs but they respond with their thoughts during the conversation. On the other hand, service leaders are active listeners, paying close attention to what they are being told and asking clarifying questions so that they can understand. This is similar to what a servant leader does. According to Anzalone, "A true servant leader would relentlessly and bravely question while listening and would show utmost respect for followers by not allowing even the slightest amount of careless or dismissive thinking to creep into the conversation."[18] This statement is also relevant for service leaders who listen openly without being dismissive of the speaker's opinion or concern but respect the speaker enough to question them for clarification.

Traditional leaders, on the other hand, may tend to focus more on transmitting than receiving the message and thereby discourage moral dialogue. What this means is that they tend to be thinking more about what they will say next rather than actually listening to what is being communicated to them. In short, they are passive listeners and in order to become a service leader they need to be active listeners. For a speaker, as shown above, this type of passive listening comes across as dismissive and uncaring.

COMMUNICATING CONCERN

It is critical to listen not just to the words but for meaning and discern why the speaker is saying what she is saying and what the situational background may be. This type of listening demonstrates to the speaker that a service leader is giving individualized consideration and is also sensitive to his needs. Referring to the previous example, this would be the distinction between listening to what a patron wants and listening for what they need. Some discussion and query is usually necessary to be able to discern what they need to use the information for and why:

> . . . you're not just hearing the words, but you're also experiencing, to some degree, what the other person is going through, what they're trying to convey, and it usually requires undivided attention. It isn't a case of listening so you can formulate an answer. It's simply trying to understand. And, it's very powerful when a person feels that someone else truly understands and is trying to understand them.[19]

When a person, whether an employee or a library patron, feels like their concerns are not being listened to or, worse, are being ignored, he can also lash out. This doesn't necessarily mean the person is going to go out and hit someone; despite the fact that he might feel like doing it, he is not really going to do this. But what he will do is lash out through disassociation with the organization.

Listening empathetically not only helps a service leader gather necessary data through feedback but it demonstrates a respect for and appreciation of others, ultimately promoting an organizational culture of respect and empowerment. The foundation of empathetic listening is respect and caring for the speaker, a priority that is conveyed in the exchange and, in doing so, creates an organizational culture that allows for clarity, understanding, caring, and empathy.[20] By doing so, a service leader empowers those she serves to be involved in the decision-making process, engages employees to share the strategic vision, and helps promote a shared governance model within the organization. She also increases motivation, job satisfaction, and organizational citizenship behaviors.

Some leaders are passive listeners who do not appear to be absorbing anything they are being told. They may not offer any type of feedback about what they are being told or even appear to be listening. As a result passive listening leaders may not only become ineffective but destructive to the organization. According to Hogan et al., "managerial incompetence in America is between 60% and 75%."[21] Bell and Smith believe that there are five factors with which leaders often struggle and that cause them to be passive listeners:

1. overassertiveness;
2. internal mental competition;
3. assumptions about the speaker;
4. assumptions about the situation; and
5. laziness.[22]

According to Bell and Smith, an average conversation occurs at the rate of 150 words per minute, but a listener has the ability to comprehend at the rate of 600 words per minute. That discrepancy allows sufficient time for additional thoughts to enter a listener's mind and may impede successful listening.[23] It is not unusual to be part of a conversation, passively listening to someone and thinking about what that person is saying while at the same time contemplating a different situation or issue. Only half of an individual's attention is on the speaker and the situation at hand, assuring that they will only remember part of the conversation and may miss critical details. For example, a library director might have the mistaken understanding that all items being purchased for a library are accompanied by cataloging records. However, it is taking too long for books to get to the patrons once received in the acquisitions department. Consequently, when the supervisor of cataloging discusses the need for more staff to help in the cataloging department, the director does not consider this to be a solution because what the supervisor is saying does not fit into what the director already believes. Hence the director does not listen to what the supervisor is saying.

Listening is a skill that can be acquired and practiced. There are a number of tools that can be employed to improve listening skills, including the following:

Listening to what is said and what is not said

Listening involves paying attention to all the information being given, not just what one hears or reads but also the nonverbal message or body language that the sender is using to transmit the information to the receiver. In order to train oneself to listen to what is being said and what is not said, the receiver must not only listen to the information being passed but also see the body language of the person transmitting this information. It is only once we hear the voice and see the speaker's body language that a service leader can begin to understand how the speaker truly feels about the information he is giving you. For example, if an employee tells you that he supports a recent decision you made but as he is telling you this does not make eye contact and shrugs his shoulders while backing away, he doesn't give the impression that he is truly supporting your decision. You can use these cues to ask additional questions to see what problems the speaker has with the current issue.

Feelings can be a large part of communication and a leader should not dismiss the speaker's feelings. Part of listening is paying attention to what is not being said. Listening for feelings from the speaker is as important as listening for the facts. Sometimes a person will say something that normally wouldn't seem important until you hear the tone of the speaker's voice. In order to truly understand what a person is saying, it is essential for a service leader to understand how the employee feels and attach the feelings to the information being given. This can be done not only by listening to the tone and rhythmic pace of a person's voice but also by seeing the person's facial expressions and hand gestures, and by making eye contact. Once a service leader has the ability to hear and see these types of emotional cues, he will have additional information to understand the complete meaning of what the speaker is trying to relay.[24]

Filtering out superfluous or repetitive information to get at the facts

It is important for a service leader to listen to the facts that the speaker is giving her. However, not all the information coming from the speaker is necessary for the leader to know. This is particularly true when the speaker becomes passionate about the topic and begins going into too much detail about the topic when only a little information may be suffice. The speaker may include both facts and feelings or assumptions—and it is critical for the listener to be able to discern which is which. Service leaders train themselves to listen for the important elements asking such questions as: why is John telling me this information, why is 380 items a minute important, why is John continuing to repeat the word *circulation* desk, why does John repeat the name of the dean of the libraries when giving me this information? By doing this a service leader can recognize and focus in on the key information needed and discard or dismiss the information that is not important.

Give signs that you are listening

The greatest compliment to another person is listening to them, really listening to and understanding what the speaker is saying. "You have to listen as if you mean it. Sit up, take a few notes, ask clarifying questions, [and] show some reaction to what is being said."[25] It is important when listening to a person to give both verbal and nonverbal acknowledgement signs such as eye contact, asking questions or making sounds to convey that you are paying attention and that you are still listening and interested in what the speaker is saying. This is still significant when you are speaking on the phone or when visual cues are absent, and as a result the person does not see any recognition on the other end of the line. The easiest way to acknowledge the speaker, whether on the phone or in a small group setting, it to pose relevant questions to the speaker or make small acknowledgements such as saying, "uh, right, ummmm, ah."

However, making noises as listening cues in large groups can become problematic because it could raise the noise level of the room to an unmanageable level and take attention away from the information being given. To avoid creating an unmanageable state, it is best during large group meetings to give the speaker visual cues instead of auditory cues. However, it is important that when you are being a responsible listener, particularly in large groups, that you don't use a nonverbal acknowledgement, such as a nod, that may come across to the speaker as agreement or support.

Listening without bias or a preset agenda

It is, of course, impossible to listen without bias or agenda, for each person receives input through their own lens. However, it is advisable to be aware of your own biases and understand that others have their own which inform their perceptions as well as what and how they choose to communicate. This is done without judging or assuming. "Ask yourself whether you are willing to change your point of view before you sit down at a meeting with staff or colleagues. Are you wedded to the way you see things? Are you going through the motions—collecting feedback on a project or on a decision only to forge ahead with a pre-existing plan of action? Are you listening only to poke holes in your colleagues' arguments?"[26]

Seek diversity of opinion

Being proactive and seeking people out to listen to their opinions and advice is key to understanding the person and your organization. There is nothing worse for an organization than to have the leader always go to the same person or group of people to seek their advice. Often the leader's choice of advisor is of like mind and tends to see the world the same way the leader does. Generally, these advisors are known throughout the organization as the chosen ones, boot lickers, or the favorites, and all too often they tend to destroy the organization because of their like-minded vision or lack of vision. Greenleaf believes that it is important "every week, [for a leader to] set aside an hour to listen to somebody who might have something to say that will be of interest. It should be a conscious practice in which all of the impulses to argue, inform, judge, and 'straighten out' the person are denied. Every response should be calculated to reflect interest, understanding, seeking for more knowledge."[27] Find that individual who is critical of the organization and listen and understand what and why they are saying what they are saying. This is how a leader can solicit diverse opinions amongst his team.

This chapter has largely focused on communication internal to a library or service organization, where employees or patrons are really the primary concern. It may appear that these priorities are in conflict when, in fact, they are not only complementary but aligned. If library leaders are not listening to their employees, showing them respect and inclusion, then what is their consideration of their users? In any service organization, such as a library, where meeting the patron's needs is the fundamental mission, listening becomes extremely important. Library literature acknowledges this importance with droves of articles analyzing patron interactions as typified by the importance of listening during the reference interview. A groundbreaking 1968 article by Robert Taylor describes the reference interview as "one of the most complex acts of human communication," in which one person must articulate what she wants when she does not really know what she wants.[28] The librarian must empathetically listen to the patron without any preconceived notions or judgments and help the patron get the information she needs even if it is not what she explicitly said she wanted. Librarians who listen in spurts or listens by only hearing words will never be able to fully understand what the patron needs. This is critical since an effective reference interview and successful outcome is collaborative between the patron and the librarian.

REFLECTIONS ON LISTENING AND BUILDING RAPPORT: TOOLS FOR DEVELOPMENT

For one full week set aside 20 minutes at the end of each day to answer the following questions:

1. Throughout the day how often was I: (a) an empathetic listener; (b) hearing words but not really listening; (c) listening in spurts?
2. For each of the above conversations, who were you listening to and what was the context of the situation?
3. For those times that you were not listening as an empathetic listener, what were you distracted with and was it as important as the person speaking?
4. For those conversations in which you were hearing words but not really listening or listening in spurts, put yourself in the speaker's shoes and try to imagine what it was like for her to speak to someone who was not listening empathetically. How does that make you feel? What are the implications of not listening to them?

NOTES

1. Kent Allen Farnsworth, *Leadership as Service: A New Model for Higher Education in a New Century* (Westport, CO: Greenwood, 2007), 54.
2. Arthur H. Bell and Dayle M. Smith, *Management Communication* (New York: Wiley, 1999), 353.

3. Ibid.

4. Don DeGraaf, Colin Tilley, and Larry Neal, "Servant-Leadership Characteristics in Organizational Life," in *Practicing Servant Leadership: Succeeding through Trust, Bravery, and Forgiveness,* eds. L.C. Spears and M. Lawrence (San Francisco, CA: Jossey-Bass, 2004), 135.

5. Fons Trompenaars and Ed Voerman, *Servant-Leadership Across Cultures* (New York: McGraw Hill, 2010); Robert K. Greenleaf, *Servant Leadership: A Journey into the Nature of Legitimate Power & Greatness* (Mahwah, NJ: Paulist, 1977); James M. Kouzes and Barry Z. Posner, *The Leadership Challenge,* 3rd ed. (San Francisco, CA: Jossey-Bass, 2002).

6. Warren Bennis and Burt Nanus, *Leaders: The Strategies for Taking Charge* (New York: Harper & Row, 1985), 17–18.

7. Don DeGraaf, Colin Tilley, and Larry Neal, "Servant-Leadership Characteristics in Organizational Life," *Practicing Servant Leadership: Succeeding through Trust, Bravery, and Forgiveness,* eds. L.C. Spears and M. Lawrence (San Francisco, CA : Jossey-Bass, 2004), 136.

8. Larry C. Spears, "The Understanding and Practice of Servant-Leadership," in Servant Leadership Research Roundtable, August 2005, www.regent.edu/acad/global/publications/sl_proceedings/2005/spears_practice.pdf.

9. Mark A. Rennaker, *Listening and Persuasion: Examining the Communicative Patterns of Servant Leadership* (Regent University, 2008), 43.

10. Gilbert W. Fairholm, *Perspectives on Leadership: From the Science of Management to Its Spiritual Heart* (Westport, CT: Quorum Books, 1998).

11. Robert F. Russell and A. Gregory Stone, "A Review of Servant Leadership Attributes: Developing a Practice Model," *Leadership and Organization Development Journal* 23, no. 3 (2002): 148–149.

12. Lyman K. Steil, Larry L. Barker, and Kittie W. Watson, *Effective Listening: Key to Your Success* (Reading, Mass.: Addison-Wesley, 1983).

13. Madelyn Burley-Allen, *Listening the Forgotten Skill: A Self-Teaching Guide,* 2nd ed. (New York: John Wiley, 1995).

14. Ibid., 13–14.

15. Ibid., 14.

16. Ibid., 142.

17. Robert K. Greenleaf, *Servant Leadership: A Journey into the Nature of Legitimate Power & Greatness* (New York, NY: Paulist Press, 2002), 313.

18. Filippa Marullo Anzalone, "Servant Leadership: A New Model for Law Library Leaders," *Law Library Journal* 99, no. 4 (2007): 798.

19. Curtis D. Beck, "Antecedents of Servant Leadership: A Mixed Methods Study," (dissertation, University of Nebraska at Lincoln, 2010), 72.

20. Madelyn Burley-Allen, *Listening: the Forgotten Skill: A Self-Teaching Guide,* 2nd ed. (New York, NY: John Wiley, 1995).

21. Robert Hogan, Gordon J. Curphy, and Joyce Hogan, "What We Know About Leadership: Effectiveness and Personality," *American Psychologist* 49, no. 6 (1994): 494.

22. Arthur H. Bell and Dayle M. Smith, *Management Communication* (New York, NY: Wiley, 1999), 354.

23. Ibid.

24. Ibid., 358.

25. National Performance Review and Vice President Albert Gore, "World-Class Courtesy: A Best Practices Report: A Report of the National Performance Review" (The Review, 1997), 8.

26. Filippa Marullo Anzalone, "Servant Leadership: A New Model for Law Library Leaders," *Law Library Journal* 99, no. 4 (2007): 798.

27. Robert Greenleaf, *On Being a Servant Leader,* eds. Don M. Frick and Larry C. Spears (San Francisco, CA: Josey-Bass, 1990), 70.

28. Robert Taylor, "Question-Negotiation and Information Seeking in Libraries," *College & Research Libraries* 29, no. 3 (May 1968): 180.

CHAPTER 5

....

BALANCING ENCOURAGEMENT
AND ACCOUNTABILITY

....

It is a shame that so many leaders spend their time pondering their rights as
leaders instead of their awesome *responsibilities* as leaders.
—*James C. Hunter*[1]

Encouragement and accountability are flip sides of the same coin: the positive support and reinforcement given to an individual to take a risk, to do something innovative or new, and the stimulus to take responsibility for such actions (or inactions) and their results. The effort to communicate this message, encouraging or critical, to make an impact on someone else, can also be interpreted as influence.

Influence is largely tied to finding out what motivates people. If an individual is attentive to what motivates someone else, she can speak to what that person finds meaningful and help him achieve it. This builds rapport and community within the organization and influence for the individual making efforts. Some might call it manipulation. Looking at what motivates individuals or what people need and employing that information to forge a connection with them may be considered strategic in a business environment but called manipulative in a public service environment. However, it may breed better communication and mutual understanding, and when it is applied for purposes of public service, results in a more effective and mutually beneficial outcome.

INFLUENCE

The concept of soft power, as developed by Joseph Nye, is similar to influence.[2] It is the use of diplomacy to achieve goals as opposed to hard power, which takes more aggressive measures. In the environment of international relations, hard power may be the use of economic sanctions or even military action; in the context of an organization, hard power may the use of raises or penalties like demotions. Nye asserted that "soft power lies in the ability to attract and persuade," but this assumes that the focus is still on service, benefiting the individual and organization.[3] It is distinctive from a more political perspective: "A Machiavellian leader would in many ways stand in a stark contrast to a servant leader. In a typical leader-follower relationship, the former subscribes to the view that the end justifies the means, whereas the latter believes that both the ends and means should be morally justifiable."[4] Service leadership and the ability to influence others come from an ethical platform. "When our policies are seen as legitimate in the eyes of others, our soft power is enhanced," and it is this platform that allows a service leader to influence others and be effective in the organization.[5]

Charan reports that 30 to 50 percent of leaders are unsuccessful in accomplishing their goals.[6] One reason for this failure may be that the leader exhibits negative behaviors that undermine her ability to be effective, such as the one mentioned above by Hunter. Although there are numerous negative leadership behaviors, such as: conceit, dishonesty, irritability, selfishness, insensitivity, and aggressiveness, research has shown that there are five common behaviors that have led leaders to fail:

1. emotional instability;
2. defensiveness;
3. lack of integrity;
4. poor communication; and
5. overestimation of their own importance and power.

PERSONAL ACCOUNTABILITY AS A LIBRARY LEADER

It may not be apparent what these behaviors have to do with encouragement and accountability, but they are actually quite relevant. Personal accountability is important to service leaders. Not only should they understand the policies and procedures that are the nuts and bolts of their organization, they should make decisions based on them. Once they model this behavior, others will follow; conversely, if a leader does not model this behavior, it sends a mixed message that might prompt confusion or feelings of inequity. Aligning action to words and modeling policies and values are critical, particularly in terms of setting standards of behavior in an organization.

All of us have known supervisors who are too busy to nurture their teams because they are consumed with trying to figure out their own job or, worse, attaining their own personal goals, such as gaining more power or attaining favor with the library director or university administration. Their self-interest is so strong that they take all the credit when their team performs a job well done and blames them when things go wrong. However, in trying to achieve their personal goals, these leaders neglect to connect with their team, resulting in a

SERVICE LEADERSHIP IN PRACTICE

Gabriel was a reference librarian with 30 years of experience working in a small academic college. Two years before Gabriel is set to retire, his library once again reorganizes and Gabriel finds himself reporting to a new supervisor, John. With this reorganization comes a new strategic plan that the reference unit must carry out. Although Gabriel was never excited about the countless number of supervisors that came before, John had already earned his respect because he was an outstanding veteran reference librarian who had worked alongside Gabriel for years. Gabriel believed that John's invaluable reference knowledge would make him a great supervisor. However, within weeks Gabriel begins to see John flip-flopping on decisions, saying one thing to one person and saying something completely different to another. Within a few months, these decisions come back to haunt the reference unit as staff members begin to feel like John is playing favorites, allowing one person to do one thing while allowing another to do something completely different. Finally, Gabriel makes an appointment with John to discuss the inconsistencies that he and the reference team have been facing. At the meeting, John becomes defensive, yelling at Gabriel and asserting that he is the boss and that Gabriel is an exempt employee and works for the institution '24 hours a day, 7 days a week.' Johns says that if Gabriel doesn't like the way he made decisions, he is free to resign. Within hours, Gabriel is sitting in the library director's office filling out a formal complaint against John. Although John was an outstanding reference librarian, that experience did not mean he would be an outstanding leader. Not only could John not control his emotions, he could not recognize his own flaws and became defensive, making it look to Gabriel that John was making decisions based on who was asking, not on the actual situation. John's attitude was that it's my way or the highway, overstepping his own authority. Had John recognized Gabriel's sincerity and been able to recognize that perhaps he (John) had made a mistake or been inconsistent in his decision-making, he might have encouraged Gabriel to feel empowered to engage in a dialogue and a constructive way to address these issues, such as drafting policies as a way to remain consistent. Instead of working on implementing the new strategic plan, the plan was set aside by the unit in order to address their leadership problems.

lack of understanding of the role that individual members of their team play in their support of the organization. This lack of understanding causes the leader to begin making errors, and these errors cause the team to lose confidence in their leader. Over time, the team will become self-protective and, consequently, lose focus on their assignment, instead concentrating more on their supervisor's lack of understanding and unpredictable behavior. This loss of support begins to distort the team's view of the entire library's leadership. Questions are raised. They may ask why the library director or university administration doesn't do something to address the incompetence of the supervisor or why they are not holding the leader accountable for his repeated errors.

The transition from employee to manager seems to be one that is less intentional or thought out than other strategic efforts. At best, there is a current position description for the manager. However, so often there no management expectations or goals, no way of getting feedback for development, and no relevant training beyond how to use the timesheet program or access the budget. Those identified for the greatness of management apparently already have the skills? Or perhaps they are born just knowing how (pursuant to trait theory). Just as there are expectations for different positions, there should be expectations for managers—and they should be explicit if not highly detailed. Just as with any other area of evaluation, there should be metrics or indicators related to performance and impact. There should be feedback, whether encouragement or accountability. It is not fair to hold an employee accountable to performance standards if they are not made explicitly known to the employee; why are managers any different? Managing personnel is largely looked upon as a soft skill—hard to measure and open to interpretation, situation, and style. As such, articulating expectations around management outcomes and behavior can avert costly misunderstandings and human resources issues.

There are numerous examples of individuals who were very effective as specialists but remarkably less so when promoted to a position of authority. It is not uncommon to hear such comments in organizations: "I remember so and so, he/she was a great cataloger but a horrible supervisor" or "He was so immature that he never encouraged me to do anything and whenever stuff hit the fan, he blamed everything on the unit, saying we were not team players instead of looking in the mirror for the true problem." At one time or another, most employees can point to a person who was elevated to the status of leader who was not effective. Known as the Peter Principle, a high performing individual may be elevated to the status of a manager and reach what is called "their own level of incompetence." These leaders (and we use the term loosely) might have demonstrated extraordinary skills as a subject selector or technical expert, and administration misunderstands this extraordinary skill as leadership or assumes that the success in one area is transferable to another. Library administration then promotes this person to be the supervisor of all subject selectors although the new supervisor may never have wanted to be a supervisor and has no leadership interest or skills whatsoever. As a result, this new supervisor is not only incompetent but also apathetic about the new positional responsibilities. She doesn't appear to be listening or encouraging her employees, and she doesn't make the necessary decisions to advance the organization. To some employees, it seems that this new supervisor is not being held accountable to the institution and that she is just filling all her time waiting for retirement. Think back, how many Deans or Directors have you had that you have said this is their retirement job. It is a little hard to swallow when employees are asked to be accountable to their actions but leaders aren't.

Have you ever sat in a meeting and heard this: "I want everyone in this room to feel empowered to make change." But when a person does show initiative, their supervisor comes down on them like a ton of bricks for not coming to him/her first with the idea. The employee is then penalized when he is reassigned to another job in a remote part of the library under the guise that his expertise is needed. That transplanted employee probably is not going to volunteer for anything in the library again, and the library likely just created another disgruntled employee who will be looking for a new job as fast as he can. Instead of encouraging this employee to continue feeling empowered, the supervisor sent the employee away, using him as an example of what not to do. However, nothing is done in a vacuum, and other employees in the organization understand what is truly happening and see this as another example of poor management. Ironically, the supervisor is not held accountable for her poor communication style but hailed as a strong leader for dealing with the rebel rouser. However, the employee's feelings may come back to haunt the supervisor eventually in the form of a grievance.

WHAT IS EMOTIONAL INTELLIGENCE?

Emotional intelligence, according to Salovey and Mayer, involves a person's capability to examine, analyze, and separate her own and others' emotions from different situations, so that she uses this new insight to guide her actions and decision making process.[7] Service leaders do this when they listen, not only to themselves but to others, colleagues, patrons, or team members. Gradually, researchers began redefining what emotional intelligence is and developing new methods for its measurement. As a result of this reexamination, Mayer et al. expanded their previous definition of emotional intelligence so that it encompassed the ability of a person to relate their emotions with other's and also correlate the significance of those emotions to specific types of situations.[8] Once this linkage was established, the person could use this information during the decision-making process to navigate the bumps of conflict found on the road ahead. This ability is necessary for an effective leader to be able to encourage their team members and facilitate an effective and productive effort. Emotions, whether they are positive or negative, are strong and lasting feelings that influence the way a person not only thinks but how he reacts. They determined whether an individual will speak up and say how they truly feel about a certain project, say nothing and disengage or approach the situation in a negative way.

In order to help people to navigate the roller coasters of their own and other people's emotions, Caruso and Salovey developed a process model that can provide service leaders with a common method to better recognize and understand an emotionally charged situation and also to manage these precarious conditions. This hierarchical process, called the emotional blueprint,[9] is made up of four related but different abilities: identifying, using, understanding, and managing emotions. A service leader should begin by correctly identifying the emotions that she is experiencing about a specific situation and distinguish them from those that others are feeling. The second step for a service leader, when employing the emotional blueprint, is to use the knowledge gained in step one by generating emotions and using them to achieve goals. Having gathered the information from the first and second step of the blueprint, a service leader can better understand the emotional situation, what causes the emotion, its progression and combinations, so that she will know what she will be facing and will be able to try to predict how the emotions of her team members may change depending on different situations. Once these three steps have been accomplished, a service leader can manage the emotional investment of various team members and factor them into decisions and behavior to help attain positive results.[10]

Service leaders are successful running their organizations when they possess emotional intelligence traits. For example, "a person strongly displaying the traits of engagement and curiosity, for instance, is likely to develop a high level of the competency that these two traits enable: influencing."[11] Certain traits or behaviors may build upon each other and result in other behaviors or competencies.

Leaders, particularly in academic institutions like libraries, are not exclusive to the library director. All too often there are others who don't necessarily have positional authority but end up being leaders within the organization simply because they can influence those around them, consequently impacting not only the library director's effectiveness but also holding the library director accountable. In a more hierarchical organization, however, service leadership behavior may be discouraged by anyone not in a position of authority. If an organization says that they value innovation and initiative, there should be encouragement to back that up. However, if in a meeting an individual is encouraged to feel empowered to make changes but is later ostracized for taking initiative, this sends an implicit message to that individual and to others in the organization that has a profound effect: people will not speak up in meetings, make suggestions, act on innovative ideas, or take risks. This effect also is true for upper library administration. Rarely do library directors work directly with every library staff member every day, even though he ultimately makes the decisions about performance evaluation and either remediation or rewards. In general there is a senior leadership team that manages the daily library functions. It is critical that these senior leaders are accountable and understand, just like the library director, the value of emotional intelligence as a way of encouraging and growing their employees.[12]

EMPOWERMENT

Empowerment is a term generally used in business literature to describe an organization's efforts to encourage all employees in the institution to participate in the decision-making process. Employees "can be empowered more by increasing their autonomy and discretionary opportunities and getting support from the higher authority for their efforts."[13] Leaders can arrange for employees who have social equity in the organization to signal their public commitment to new goals. This sort of encouragement by fellow employees can help move the process along for the organization. However, the key is that a service leader must also be held accountable by employees for communicating the new goals, and a service leader must hold the employees accountable to upward feedback.

Individuals embrace empowerment practices if they want to encourage their employee's participation in the organization so that it can be successful. Service leaders have their employees engage in empowering situations relevant to their interest and experience, but may also be growth opportunities. However, the opportunities should be relevant to the experience and interest of the employee. Asking a cataloger who has never worked a public service desk for her opinion on virtual reference software is neither helpful to the organization nor very concerned about her experience and engagement in the organization. It would be more effective to encourage the cataloger to participate in decision-making issues related to her area and level of expertise. She would then have the acknowledgement that her expertise was both known and valued, and she would feel some investment in the question being explored. Encouraging participation is critical, but only when there is an understanding of the reason for being asked. However, in order for a library to be successful, library leaders must also empower their users; after all, they know what they want better than library staff does. Services such as patron-driven acquisitions, for example, empower users to make decisions about the future of the library's collection. Usability studies organized by library leaders are one way to empower library patrons to have a say in how the library looks and how it runs. Such patron feedback also holds libraries accountable to ensure that the desires of the users are heard.

Encouraging empowerment goes beyond just active employee participation in an organization's decision-making process. It also encompasses giving authority and autonomy to an employee or employees so that they can accomplish a goal for the organization. A service leader trusts that the authority they have given to an employee was not given in vain. At the same time, service leaders must give the employee the autonomy needed to get the task done. That doesn't mean walking away from the employee once he has taken on the project and not checking in once in a while to make sure progress is being made and the employee doesn't need anything. When an employee is entrusted to lead a project, service leaders need to continue to be supportive of the employee's ability to get the project completed and must learn to lead from behind. Leading from behind gives the employee the autonomy needed to complete the assignment. When a leader checks in once in a while, it doesn't mean micromanaging the employee to the point where they are not allowing the employee the opportunity or encouragement to lead. All too often employees complain about their supervisor's inability to trust their knowledge and ability to complete job responsibilities. Some supervisors take over the employee's responsibilities without giving sufficient time to complete the assignment.

Researchers such as Yukl have examined the consequences of empowerment and discovered that there are both possible benefits and costs to this management practice. Some benefits of empowerment are that employees feel:

- a stronger commitment not only to the task at hand or team but also to the organization, which can result in increased quality of customer service;
- increased initiative, enthusiasm, and productivity, particularly when faced with obstacles; and
- an increase in job satisfaction, resulting in less employee turnover and increased morale.[14]

Although empowerment is often seen in a positive light, service leaders need to recognize that there are potential costs to the organization if they do empower their employees to make decisions. Yukl believes that higher costs could be attributed to:

- recruiting skilled employees with leadership abilities;
- increased financial cost for professional development classes to aid employees to become leaders;
- bad or incorrect decisions being made by some employees;
- resistance by some employees who believe that others are being favored; and

- opposition by middle managers who feel their positional authority is being threatened.[15]

Just as encouragement is balanced with accountability in terms of feedback, there is also the balance in terms of what individuals take responsibility for and what they choose not to engage on. Lueneburger asserts that: "There are two kinds of problems: My problems, and not-my-problems. What you are talking about is not my problem. Figure it out."[16] This sounds similar to the whine (yes, I meant to use the word whine) of "That is not my job" and an abdication of responsibility which undermines the service ethic. However, "for those who seek to be effective influencers, the problems of others, their challenges and aspirations, are pay dirt."[17]

Understanding what others need, serving them, builds rapport, community, and shared purpose, and in helping them achieve their goals, they are empowered. However, there is an instance in which one should not take on another's problem—that is, when taking on their problem, the leader takes their power. This situation should be avoided, particularly when people are trying to abdicate responsibility or when the experience of solving their own issue will help them grow.

Not unrelated to engagement and setting personal boundaries of responsibility is the concept of work-life balance. While respecting an individual's privacy and affirming that their personal life is personal, there should also be balance of concern for the person as an individual: "The servant leader appreciates the professional, personal, and spiritual dimensions of each person's life outside of the tangible everyday efforts of the individual in the workplace."[18] There are times that serving an individual or helping an employee may seem like it is compromising the organization as a whole; however, organizations can afford to take the long-term perspective and ultimately an investment in or accommodation for an individual will benefit the organization and its culture.

SOCIAL AND PROCEDURAL JUSTICE

Not unrelated to culture is the concept of justice. While justice is generally associated with the legal system and dependent on an ethical framework, it also manifests in organizations at various levels. Social justice, particularly, addresses fairness within a society (or organization) particularly as it relates to benefits, rights, and opportunities. More specifically, procedural justice describes evenhandedness in how processes, such as promotions and development, are employed. Within procedural justice is distributive justice, which looks at the equity of rewards, benefits, and opportunities.

According to Kontakos, "fairness strives to make the employees' place of work better and has become more than just adequate pay, benefits, and opportunities. The thought is that if an organization treats its employees well, they will give back as much or more in terms of both physical and emotional commitment."[19]

Not every manager or staff member will support the principles of service leadership, and this is why the management characteristic of justice plays a key role. During an organizational change, team members have little to no time for a leader's political agenda. The team needs a leader who will communicate clearly to them and not cloud the change message with what-if suppositions and possibilities. This is particularly crucial when not all members of the team have bought into the new goals. What service leaders need to do is be accountable to their team and encourage them to feel comfortable speaking up and challenging the leader. However, this accountability goes two ways; not only does a service leader need to hold herself accountable to her employees, she must also hold the employees accountable to the organization. For example, after a service leader has done everything to help a change-resistant staff member cope with the change over time, if the person remains resistant, it is time for the leader to talk with the staff member to determine whether he should leave the organization. As discussed in previous chapters, it is important for a leader to be true to herself as well as others. If an employee is unhappy, then it is the responsibility of the leader to help him find his way, even if his way is out the door.

One of the most important factors affecting motivation in an organization is fair treatment of employees by their leader. Employees value fairness from their boss, and when they believe that they are not being treated fairly, their job performance suffers. According to Wren, "Followers are said to be most satisfied when they believe that what they put into an activity or job and what they get out of it are roughly equivalent to what others put into and get out of it."[20]

In the following scenario, the employee is facing what is called a distributive justice issue. Distributive justice "refers to the perceived fairness of the amounts of compensation employees receive."[21] Service leaders need to be cognizant of employees' concerns about fairness because it will affect their job performance and will create an organizational culture of distrust and frustration. However, distributive justice issues are just the tip of the iceberg for employees. Procedural justice, for example, is becoming more and more prevalent. According to McFarline and Sweeney, "procedural justice refers to the perceived fairness of the means used to determine those amounts"[22] of compensation an employee receives. This is prevalent when procedures are written down but ignored by library administration. Service leaders must communicate decisions to their employees so that they understand why decisions were made, and they must follow correct organizational procedures and processes. Imagine for a moment that a call goes out to nominate a team for a specific award. The procedures sent around to everyone

SERVICE LEADERSHIP IN PRACTICE

John has been working for the library for six months. He is asked to work in a team that needs to complete a difficult and time-sensitive project. John soon discovers that his team members are not equipped to handle the project. Not only do they not understand the problem, but they also don't have the know-how to complete it. As a result, John spends most of his time explaining the issues to the team. Soon John realizes that in order to complete the project on schedule, he will need to take the lead and take a lot of the project home. When John explains what he needs to do to the team, they agree with John. When the project is completed successfully, John discovers that regardless of all the extra time and hard work that he put into the project, another member of his team was rewarded with a $500 bonus for working extra hard work to complete the project. When John approaches other members of the team and asks for clarification, a team member says, "Allen is the boss's favorite. He always gets the bonuses." How do you think this makes John feel? Do you believe that he will be motivated to work hard again to complete a time sensitive project? Probably not

who wishes to nominate a team clearly state that the nominations must be in to library administration by Thursday. The day after the nominations close, a nomination for the library administration team is sent in and is accepted by the library leader. Is this fair? How do you think the employees would feel about this? Justice issues, regardless if they are distributive or procedural, lead employees to believe that other employees are being favored. Favoritism creates feelings of resentment and an organizational culture of hostility and mistrust not only toward the leader but also toward the person who the employees view as being favored. Saks believes that an employee's perception of fairness and justice are two things that can be directly associated with an employee's engagement at work.[23] In this type of environment, employee retention is low and turnover is high. Service leaders hold themselves accountable to the procedures and policies of the library because they will lose an employee's trust and work effort if they do not.

Larson and Murtadha state that "our institutions mirror our society."[24] This rings true every time we open our iPads to read our local newspaper. Across the screen we read stories of arrests for political corruption, bullying, racism, sexual harassment, and discrimination. Today, people seem resigned to the fact that these things happen, and they do little, if anything, to undo the injustice because they believe there is nothing they can do about it. Today people have accepted injustice in their life, and when the few rise up and fight this injustice, they become outcasts of the organization, destined to be ignored and labelled rabble-rousers by their colleagues. Service leaders, however, are the rabble-rousers of organizations. They tend not only to question but to challenge the status quo of the social injustices. Service leaders continually reach for greater opportunity and justice for all.[25] Service leaders understand that the only way to make a change and end social injustice in the workplace is to hold themselves accountable to take action.

Workplace bullying is an example of social injustice. Devonish defines workplace bullying as "situations where a person repeatedly and over a period of time is exposed to negative acts (i.e., constant abuse, offensive remarks or teasing, ridicule or social exclusion) on the part of coworkers, supervisors, or subordinates."[26] This type of negative and destructive behavior creates a hostile work environment for the targeted employee, who can feel threatened and humiliated by these damaging actions. In an effort to protect themselves, targeted employees often begin to isolate themselves from other people in their organization. Rarely do they speak up in a meeting to voice their opinion and or dissent. Teresa Daniel states,

> The physical or emotional health (and sometimes both) of employees working in organizations where these types of actions are taking place are often severely impacted. In addition, the confidence of the targeted employee is frequently so destroyed by the repeated negative actions that they lack even the courage necessary to leave such a toxic environment. Instead, they find themselves trapped in a world of psychological abuse—targets of a phenomenon that had been labeled *workplace bullying.*[27]

Most people who are targets of bullies often do not report the problem because they fear that they will be retaliated against. However, when grievances are filed against the perpetrator, the offender is often shocked. According to a 2007 survey, 53 percent of employees in the U.S. workplace have experienced workplace bullying and 45 percent of the employees have stated that this has interfered with their ability to do their jobs.[28] Adding to this situation and reflecting back on accountability, other employees are witnessing bad behavior. Often they wonder why administration allows this to keep happening and keep silent about what they witness in fear that since the administration has done nothing to stop the bullying behavior it is condoning it. Adding to their stress if they say anything about what they witnessed or experienced, is the concern that they may be bullied next. In order to have a productive and motivated team, employees need to feel safe in their work environment. They need to trust that they have distributive, procedural and social justice in the workplace and that service leaders will make that happen. In order to achieve this safe environment, service leaders must continue to encourage their employees to speak up and also their employee relations unit (or more commonly called HR units) to support rather than discourage employees from seeking remediation and filing grievances. In addition, employee services or the personnel department needs to investigate employee turnover to see why the employee is leaving. Employee services must also recognize and support an employee when they are voluntarily or involuntarily leaving their position. As stated above, service leaders will not keep employees who are not performing their job responsibilities satisfactorily, but this is only after they have done everything to help that employee be successful in the organization. For this reason, timely and specific constructive and positive feedback is a necessity. People can only learn from their mistakes if they know that they did wrong and are able to take responsibility. Thus, they can learn from their mistakes and correct them. A lack of feedback for negative behaviors or issues in performance will result in no change in future behavior. The lack of feedback also have implications for encouraging positive behaviors: related to extinction theory, no acknowledgment of positive performance often results in the employee seeing no incentive to continue the positive behavior.

REFLECTIONS ON ENCOURAGEMENT AND ACCOUNTABILITY: TOOLS FOR DEVELOPMENT

1. Make an appointment with your supervisor to discuss their expectations of you and your expectations of them. Then discuss how they will hold you accountable for their expectations and how you will hold them accountable for theirs.

2. Think back over the last six months. Have you witnessed any injustice (distributive, procedural, or social) in your library? List each one you witnessed and the type of injustice it was. Now, next to each, write what you did (if anything) to address this injustice. Now reflect back on why you did or did not address the injustice. What do you think that says about you and your institution?

3. Using what you have learned about yourself and your institution from the second exercise, in the next month speak out, just once, when you recognize an injustice occurring. After you speak out, assess how it makes you feel and how you were viewed by your fellow team members and library administration?

4. At the beginning of the next big project encourage one of your team members to take the reins. Hold yourself accountable and have the team hold you accountable for supporting your team member but not micromanaging him. Now watch and see how the new team leader

embraces the challenge and how the team comes together to support one another.

NOTES

1. James C. Hunter, *The Servant: A Simple Story About the True Essence of Leadership* (New York, NY: Random House, 2012), 63–64.

2. Joseph S. Nye, *Soft Power: The Means to Success in World Politics* (New York: NY: Public Affairs, 2004).

3. Ibid.

4. Sen Sendjaya and Brian Cooper, "Servant Leadership Behaviour Scale: A Hierarchical Model and Test of Construct Validity," *European Journal of Work and Organizational Psychology* 20, no. 3 (2011): 421.

5. Joseph S. Nye, *Soft Power: The Means to Success in World Politics* (New York: NY: Public Affairs, 2004), x.

6. Ram Charan, "Why CEOs Fail," *Fortune* 139 no. 12 (1999): 68–75.

7. Peter Salovey and John D. Mayer, "Emotional Intelligence," *Imagination, Cognition and Personality* 9, no. 3 (1989–90): 186–187.

8. John Mayer, et al., "Emotional Intelligence as a Standard Intelligence", *Emotion* 1, no. 3 (2001): 232–242.

9. David R. Caruso and Peter Salovey, *The Emotionally Intelligent Manager: How to Develop and Use the Four Key Emotional Skills of Leadership* (San Francisco, CA: Jossey-Bass, 2004), 24.

10. Susan A. Kornacki and David R. Caruso, "A Theory-Based, Practical Approach to Emotional Intelligence Training: Ten Ways to Increase Emotional Skills," in *Applying Emotional Intelligence: A Practitioner's Guide*, eds. Joseph Ciarrochi and John D. Mayer (New York, NY: Psychology Press, 2007), 55.

11. Christoph Lueneburger, *A Culture of Purpose: How to Choose the Right People and Make the Right People Choose You* (San Francisco, CA: Jossey-Bass, 2014), 5.

12. Patricia A. Kreitz, "Leadership and Emotional Intelligence: A Study of University Library Directors and Their Senior Management Teams," *College & Research Libraries* 70, no. 6 (2009): 531–554.

13. Bernard M. Bass, *Bass & Stogdill's Handbook of Leadership: Theory, Research, and Managerial Applications,* 3rd ed. (New York, NY: The Free Press, 1990), 213.

14. Gary Yukl, *Leadership in Organizations*, 6th ed. (Upper Saddle River, NJ: Prentice Hall, 2006), 108.

15. Ibid.

16. Christoph Lueneburger, *A Culture of Purpose: How to Choose the Right People and Make the Right People Choose You* (San Francisco, CA: Jossey-Bass, 2014), 31.

17. Ibid.

18. Filippa Marullo Anzalone, "Servant Leadership: A New Model for Law Library Leaders," *Law Library Journal* 99, no. 4 (2007): 802.

19. Anne-Marie Kontakos, "Employee Engagement and Fairness in the Workplace," *Center for Advanced Human Resources Studies* (2007), 18, www.ilr.cornell.edu/cahrs/research/whitepapers/upload/EmployeeEngagement_FairWorkplace.pdf.

20. J. Thomas Wren, *The Leader's Companion: Insights on Leadership Through the Ages* (New York, NY: The Free Press, 1995), 331.

21. Dean B. McFarlin and Paul D. Sweeney, "Distributive and Procedural Justice as Predictors of Satisfaction with Personal and Organizational Outcomes," *Academy of Management Journal* 35, no. 3 (1992): 626.

22. Ibid.

23. Alan M. Saks, "Antecedents and Consequences of Employee Engagement," *Journal of Managerial Psychology* 21, no. 7 (2006): 600–619.

24. Colleen L. Larson and Khaula Murtadha, "Leadership for Social Justice," *Yearbook of the National Society for the Study of Education* 101, no. 1 (2002): 134.

25. Ibid., 135.

26. Dwayne Devonish, "Workplace Bullying, Employee Performance and Behaviors: The Mediating Role of Psychological Well-Being," *Employee Relations* 35, no. 6 (2013): 630.

27. Teresa A. Daniel, *Stop Bullying at Work: Strategies and Tools for HR and Legal Professionals* (Alexandria, Va.: Society for Human Resource Management, 2009), 1.

28. Ibid., 9.

CHAPTER 6

INNOVATION AND EVOLVING SERVICE

We keep moving forward, opening new doors, and doing new things,
because we're curious and curiosity keeps leading us down new paths.
—*Walt Disney*[1]

The quote above is attributed to Walt Disney when he spoke about his secret of successful innovation. He continued with "we call it Imagineering—the blending of creative imagination and technical know-how."[2] Disney knew that in a service organization, service, not technology, should be the driving force behind innovation; in fact, the Disney philosophy is now considered the gold standard of service, and his company even provides service training to organizations, both public and private.

Technology often is the driver for a new library service simply because there is something new and flashy. Particularly, when library users state that they want to see this technology used, because it is the next best thing; however, the actual application of the technology may be limited in its benefit to library services. Libraries using blogs is one such example. Service is about who is being served and making sure that they get what they need, which may be different from what they want. This differentiates libraries and other service institutions from corporations and organizations, which may focus on the transactional relationship and the bottom line.

Ultimately, service organizations, including academic libraries, are driven by the public good; they are for the benefit of the public. In an oversimplified model, service, as framed by patrons' needs, is the driver; innovative and strategic thinking and shared vision show the route, and strategic planning creates the map. Following that metaphor, technology may be the vehicle. Libraries are dependent on technology to be the platform on which they provide service and convey expertise; technology is completely embedded in library services and operations. Since libraries are so dependent on technology for many of their services and operations and many patrons are demanding the next best thing, it is not uncommon for service to take a back seat to technology, particularly because technology is so eye-catching and sensational. When this happens, services are introduced into libraries because of a hot new trend; the change initiated by the library leader tends to focus more on the implementation of the technology rather than how it might enhance the service itself which has the potential to create a management situation in the organization and the inability to meet patron expectations. This chapter examines innovation from a service leadership standpoint. It will highlight how the term *innovation* is often used synonymously with *creativity* and *vision*, although for a service leader all three terms are considered distinct from one another. It will focus on how a service leader distinguishes these terms and the relationships between them during the change-management process.

CREATIVITY, VISION, AND INNOVATION

New services are critical to any service organization in order to keep evolving with the environment and to stay relevant, and libraries are no exception. In business parlance, the priority is called maintaining a competitive advantage. According to Grönfeldt and Strother, there are eight motivating factors that lead service corporations to develop or design new services. They are:

- financial goals—profit, market share, or revenue;
- competitive action;
- globalization;
- technology;
- regulation or deregulation—companies can enter into markets not open to them before or vice versa;
- elimination of professional association restrictions;
- growth of franchising; and
- balancing supply and demand.[3]

This model is also relevant for public organizations with service missions. Innovations benefit libraries by breathing life into old services, enhancing the success of current library service, and increasing patron loyalty to the library itself by keeping pace with their expectations and needs. Service leaders recognize the intrinsic value of service innovations. In order to achieve their goal, they not only encourage innovation among their team but reward it through multiple avenues, such as promotion, financial compensation, or recognition of a job well done. However, as stated above, innovation is often used synonymously with creativity and vision even though they are distinct. Creativity is the intellectual process of envisioning new knowledge or generating new ideas or goals for an organization, or "the ability to think about ideas or do things in non-routine ways."[4] Vision, on the other hand "is a desired future state: this is the basis for directing the change effort."[5] In short, vision is often seen as the big picture. Innovation, on the other hand, is the practical application or development of these ideas. In order to understand these distinct differences, we will examine them separately below.

According to Hughes et al., creativity is made up of the following seven components:

1. Synthetic ability is a skill that helps team members see ideas in unique ways by recognizing original patterns and their links.
2. Analytic intelligence is a skill that helps team members to measure and evaluate library goals and solutions.
3. Practical intelligence is a skill that supplies team members with a foundation of applied knowledge and experience that helps them to develop innovative results.
4. Thinking style is a team member's preferred method of employing their individual competencies to either develop, improve, or adapt products or processes.
5. Personality factors impact the creativity of a library employee. A creative person is seen as being inquisitive, open minded, self confident, energetic, daring, independent, and impetuous, while those who lack these qualities are considered less creative.
6. Intrinsically motivated library employees are seen as being more creative when they feel challenged by the need to solve an issue.
7. Library employees are also impacted by environmental factors: for example, those who have boring jobs coupled with a micromanager who does not support independent thought are less creative.[6]

Unlike the traditional hierarchical library leaders, service leaders do not feel that they always need to be the creative force behind their team. Instead they work to construct a service organization where all members of their team are given the opportunity and encouragement to be creative. After all, according to Hughes et al., "innovations have their roots in ideas developed by people closest to a problem or opportunity."[7] The people closest to the problems are the employees themselves, who are the integral part of the workload process. Dewey added that, "Individuals willing to experiment without precise outcomes are valued in the new public services environment. Innovative librarians can help others to think more creatively and broadly regarding library programs and services, even if they do not hold official leadership positions."[8]

Adding to this supportive environment, service leaders praise team members when initiatives are successful—and even when they are not—because they understand that it is through successes and failures that the team's creativity will grow and new initiatives will be realized. It is true that in today's society success is celebrated and failure is ignored or, worse, censured and used as an example of what not to do. Just look at today's news: Movie stars are celebrated for the success of their performance on the big screen. Medical researchers are deemed successful when they discover a cure for premature hair loss. Politicians are celebrated when they successfully win an election and enter the political arena. In all these cases, it is easy to see why the individuals are celebrated, but what about the steps it took for the movie star to get to that successful performance and how many research experiments failed before the medical researcher achieved that final success? If these successful people were chastised for failing before achieving their successes, do you think they might have given up and gone onto something else? Think of it in terms of Thomas Edison's failures when he was inventing the light bulb. A reporter asked, "Isn't it a shame that with the tremendous amount of work you have done you haven't been able to get any results?" Edison turned on me like a flash, and with a smile replied: 'Results! Why, man, I have gotten a lot of results! I know several thousand things that won't work.' Edison did not get discouraged; he saw his failures as a discovery or learning experience as he found 1,000 ways not to make a light bulb. Edison saw that it is through our failures that we innovate.[9]

If a person is chastised and punished for failing, how fast do you think that person is going to turn their back on innovation and just do the bare minimum to get by? When both success and failure are celebrated, however, the team members will develop a sense of trust, not only in one another but also in their leader. Consequently, the organizational culture, along with the feelings of an employee toward his organization, has a significant bearing on creativity and the extent of innovation that transpires within the library. An employee feels that he is part of an innovative organization when that organization not only nurtures innovation but promotes and fosters a constructive approach towards solving problems, not seeing these issues as problems but as possible opportunities. A service leader is willing to examine current services to see what is and isn't working and embraces change, regardless of the extent of the change (small or large). They are supported by their team because they not only admit to making mistakes or acknowledge failures but don't cast blame. Instead, they use these mistakes and failures as a learning opportunity for employees and thereby create a learning organization. Members of a learning organization learn as they investigate current problems and become proactive, rather than reactive, in identifying and addressing possible future issues and opportunities for the organization.[10] If a library creates a learning organization, the library administration recognizes that not all ideas come from the administration but rather from the employees on the front lines. As the creative learning organization develops, intellectual stimulation becomes its foundation. Members of the service team do not fear discovering problems but rather embrace the intellectual query and are stimulated with searching out possible solutions.

Haass argues that when developing a vision a leader needs to "think ahead from looking back."[11] This goes beyond thinking about how to progress from where you are and involves considering where you want to end up and what steps will get you there. This big-picture thinking is not meant to advocate a Machiavellian perspective. Actions in the process or efforts should align with the end in mind but they should also be consistent with personal and organizational values. That said, the idea that it is the journey, not the destination is also not desirable in organizations; just think of someone wandering aimlessly.

If articulated correctly, a vision can instill in library employees a feeling of purpose and a drive to reach their goal. When service leaders articulate an inspiring vision, employees are drawn away from the way things used to be done or are currently being done and are motivated to achieve the library's vision. A vision creates a sense of belonging among its team members because they are able to tie what they do for the organization with how it fits into the vision.

Articulating vision can be difficult and dangerous for a person's career, even when the vision is shared and supported by the team and leader. The reason why it is dangerous, according to Senge, is that "Shared visions compel courage so naturally that people don't even realize the extent of their courage. Courage is simply doing whatever is needed in pursuit of the vision."[12] However, imagine what it would be like trying to articulate a new vision to a team of reference librarians where the success of the implementation of the vision rests on librarians no longer helping patrons at a reference desk. In a library where both staff and patrons have supported the reference desk model, sending a clearly articulated message to the team would be essential to the survival of the vision. However, having a vision and having employees committed to the vision are two different things. The commitment of the team to achieve the vision depends on the team's trust in the service leader. When a leader's statements and actions are not consistent, then the team is less likely to support the vision. However, when a service leader's actions and statements are consistent, then the team is more likely to be committed to the vision.[13]

According to Russell, "a good vision is not based on 'egocentric ambition' (many tyrants possess a vision), rather it incorporates a value system that protects and promotes organizational integrity, while encouraging 'learning and adaptation.'"[14] Service leaders base their decision-making on their value system while being cognizant of the values of others around them in the organization.

Innovation is the practical application or development of creativity and vision. In order to be creative, a service leader must not only have a vision but be able to articulate that vision to her team. As stated above, innovation is not necessarily reliant on the creativity of a service leader alone. It is not unusual to have a creative team or a group in the organization that works incredibly well together, inspiring innovation in one another. However, without the support and encouragement of a service leader who recognizes the importance of the innovative team, rarely can the innovation be articulated or supported in the organization. But creativity should not be confused with competence or expertise. An individual may have 25 years of experience in constructing shelves and be very experienced and proficient at the task, but he may not possess the creativity and vision needed to design new shelving solutions. Service leaders are able to articulate what they know and what they don't know.

As innovations are introduced into the service organization, change occurs. Change is the process of adjustment or evolution in an organization. Darwin's theory, evolve or die, does not mean that the strong survive but that those who are best able to adapt to their environment will prevail. "According to Darwin's *Origin of Species,* it is not the most intellectual of the species that survives; it is not the strongest that survives; but the species that survives is the one that is able best to adapt and adjust to the changing environment in which it finds itself."[15]

People will also be more creative when they are intrinsically motivated or feel challenged by the subject matter or problem itself.[16] Creative people are more likely to focus attention on solving the problem at hand, not on the need to meet deadlines, make money, or impress others.[17] It is readily apparent, with the continuing rapid change in technology and globalization, that change is, ironically, a permanent factor in library service and librarianship. When change is necessary, libraries are going to be impacted in any number of ways, including library processes, organizational structure, transition in positional roles, and systems and technology integration.

As we all know, the driver of change itself is generally either a reactionary measure that a library takes when it is faced with an internal or external problem or a proactive measure that library leaders take when they see an opportunity that could further the organization. The change initiative can be as complex as the need for an academic library to align itself with the strategic mission of its university or as simple as making a decision to stop giving pencils out at the reference desk. Regardless of how complicated or easy the change may seem, one thing is for sure—the success or failure of the change will depend on how the library leader manages it. It is important to note that the innovative spirit, sometimes called the entrepreneurial spirit, seems to be a rare attribute in libraries.[18] If that is the case and librarians and their leaders continue to be passive, allowing libraries to drift along without giving proper attention to the need for more innovation and entrepreneurial spirit that is responsive to the changes in society, then libraries will indeed face a crisis, not only in library leadership but also in relevancy to their patrons.[19]

Grönfeldt and Strother have suggested that there are five ways that a service leader can redesign services either to increase customers' benefits or to reduce the cost of service: self-service, direct service, preservice, bundled service, and physical service.[20] The context that they provide is business-oriented, but the model has applications for public organizations such as libraries:

1. Self-service is defined as a service method of engaging library patrons in the service process so that they gain some control over the time they spend using the service as well as access to the service itself. Librarians have become very good at developing and utilizing self-service in libraries. Self-checkout machines are a perfect example of this. Not only have these machines allowed patrons to check out library items without having to wait in the lines at the checkout counter, they have allowed libraries to reduce the hours of operation of their circulation desk, which now directs patrons to the machines.

2. Direct service models are those that no longer require the library patron to come to the physical library but rather bring the library service to the patron. Services such as chat reference, document delivery, and electronic resources allow the patron to visit the library virtually from the comfort of their own office or home. Reference help can now be sought virtually in real time, material delivered via interlibrary loan to an office or desktop, saving the patron's time.

3. Preservice models attempt to enhance the initial contact between the library and the library patron so that the experience is enriched as the patron progresses through the service process. Some academic libraries send information packets out to new incoming students. These packets have detailed information about how to register as a library user, and they identify what services are available to students when they first arrive on campus.

4. Bundled service, often viewed as a dirty word in the library field, is a model that is created to improve customer value and convenience by grouping services together. Bundled service is generally a corporate model, such as internet access, phone, and security services; in the context of libraries, it is packages of journal subscriptions or databases (with the library as the customer providing access for their patrons). This model is less relevant for library services to patrons because, as with most public organizations, while there may be a suite of services, integrated or not, there is nothing compelling patrons to use all of them; they can pick and choose what they want.

5. Physical service, the focus of many libraries, looks at the library's physical space in an attempt to create a positive impact on customers' experiences while in the library building. For example, academic libraries

are moving low-use library materials to off-site storage in an attempt to make more useable patron space, such as study rooms, visual labs, and writing centers.[21]

These models describe various ways of delivering services, but much of the innovation in libraries is related to new services that start with individuals who are stimulated by a service opportunity and initiate projects. In order for librarians to think more like an innovative entrepreneur, Pinchot devised ten rules for entrepreneurs to follow to achieve their goals:

1. "Come to work each day willing to be fired.
2. Circumvent any orders aimed at stopping your dream.
3. Do any job needed to make your project work, regardless of your job description.
4. Find people to help you.
5. Follow your intuition about the people you choose, and work only with the best.
6. Work underground as long as you can—publicity triggers the corporate immune mechanism.
7. Never bet on the race unless you are running in it.
8. Remember it is easier to ask for forgiveness than for permission.
9. Be true to your goals, but be realistic about the ways to achieve them.
10. Honor your sponsors."[22]

Although some of these rules are more challenging to follow than others, those who embrace them will help libraries achieve their desired goals by introducing new services. According to Grönfeldt and Strother:

> The development of new services is very important as a driver of competitive advantage for any service organization. What usually motivates a new service development or design are (a) financial goals–profit, market share, or revenue; (b) competitive action; (c) globalization; (d) technology; (e) regulation or deregulation—companies can enter into markets not open to them before or vice versa; (f) eliminating of professional association restrictions; (g) growth of franchising; and (h) balancing supply and demand.[23]

CHANGE MANAGEMENT AND STRATEGIC THINKING

Leban and Stone define change management as "a systematic process whereby an organization responds to and adapts to the forces in its micro-and macroenvironment in order to increase its effectiveness and ensure its survival."[24] However, the success or failure of a change initiative within a library rests with the organization's employees. If employees favor the change, then their attitude and behavior toward the change will be positive. However, if employees do not favor the change, then their manners toward the change will be negative and they will exhibit change-resistance behaviors that slow, if not stop, the change initiative. When creating a change-management process, service leaders create a plan to reach the library's goal, a key component of which focuses on the library's employees and how to help those who are not on board with the change. Service leaders achieve this goal by focusing on listening to why their employees are resisting change and also by trying to understand and mediate their concerns in order to change their behaviors.[25]

In an academic library (and in the university at large) getting academics together is not unlike herding cats. However, it is easier if they all *want* to go in the same direction. There are a couple of ways to achieve this: like cats, they can either all run away from something, (usually inspired by fear) ultimately to scatter, hide, or fight back; or they can all run toward something that is attracting them—a goal, a vision, or a shared effort.

> Change *leadership* . . . starts with the willingness to stand up for a point of view that requires action in close quarters, even if you are the only one in the room advocating for that particular thing (indeed especially then). Leading change means not only presenting your view to others but also transforming those people into multipliers of the message from their own vantage points.[26]

Failure to address employees' concerns about change will slow the change down, if not cause it to fail and possibly create an organizational crisis needing a crisis-management intervention. Organizational crisis is defined as "a low-probability, high-impact event that threatens the viability of the organization and is characterized by ambiguity of cause, effect, and means of resolution, as well as by a belief that decisions must be made swiftly."[27]

In the following vignette, Brian faces a potential crisis in the library organization since a large number of library staff members are not only upset with the e-mail/calendar change but are refusing to use it. What the library now faces is something that could threaten to harm the library operations and its daily function. Although Brian had used creativity in addressing the issue, he did not speak with the library staff members and explain that the old e-mail system did not have the calendaring function that they needed to perform the job duties. If he had, he might have averted the crisis. As mentioned in chapter 4, it is during this communication stage that service leaders build a rapport based on trust with

SERVICE LEADERSHIP IN PRACTICE

Brian, a veteran local area network administrator, was asked to lead the selection and implementation of a new e-mail service for a medium-size academic library. The library needed a new e-mail service that would allow the library to use a state-of-the-art calendaring system that their old e-mail system lacked and that was needed by the library staff. Brian began investigating the different types of e-mail and calendar services and made a decision about which one to purchase. He assumed that the decision to move to the new e-mail system was amicable and that everyone was on board with the change. However, at no time did Brian involve the users in the decision-making process. Within days of implementation, Brian was approached repeatedly in the halls by a large number of library staff members complaining that the new system was too hard to use, that they would not use the new system and would continue using the old system. The staff members let Brian know that at no time were they consulted in the choosing of the system, nor were they given the opportunity to participate and test the calendaring system, which they believe did not have the functions they needed in a calendar system. What seemed to start out as a simple change initiative had now developed into a potential crisis situation because Brian did not consider getting the library employees' buy-in when he made his decision.

those being affected by the change. Often this can be done by communicating with the affected community to get input about what they actually need instead of what is assumed they need. Once the true problem has been identified, it is time for a service leader to work collaboratively together with those who are affected by the change to find a solution. It is during this stage that people work together to discover new ways of solving their problem. By working together the group develops a bond and becomes invested in making the solution work for the organization. Once the problem and solution have been identified, the implementation of the agreed-upon solution begins. It is imperative that all the phases of the change-management process occur. Without the buy-in from those affected by the change, the solution will have a greater chance of failing because the employees will view the solution with apathy or, worse, resistance.

This is also true when managing change that impacts library patrons. In order to identify the needs of all who could be affected by change, service leaders should reach out to the impacted community and engage them in dialogue. Managing change is a multifaceted process and cannot be done in a vacuum. There are a number of ways to reach out to these groups. One way is through focus groups. A second way is to send out surveys that encourage direct feedback.

Service leaders are committed to patron service, building on their desire to serve and help their library patrons. But this value presumes that the foundation of service leadership is concern and respect for the people they work with and for the people they serve. The desire to serve can foster a more diverse climate, not just in terms of gender, ethnicity, etc., but in terms of viewpoint, communication style, and personal values as the service leader strives to understand and connect to the library's internal and external environment. There are a number of theories that argue that many diverse points of view and opinions make an organization better, particularly when a person disagrees with the norm since it triggers a service leader to rethink her view along with the view held by the library. By gathering feedback and respecting the opinions of others, libraries are less likely to be trapped in group-think and will continue to evolve and flourish, introducing new ideas into the organization.

The encouragement of open and honest feedback sends a signal to others in and out of the library that it is okay to disagree with library administration and that their views are not only wanted but valued. Eventually this encouragement to air dissenting views will be reflected in how employees treat library patrons when they express unhappiness about service they receive. Employees will no longer view these patrons as difficult but rather come to encourage and value them for their help in creating a better service. Everyone has that one patron, the one that needs special handling or that will run straight past the library director to the university president. Often it is a distinguished professor with a Nobel Prize under his belt and a strong opinion on what constitutes service in the library. In many instances this individual is tolerated and placated and, if at all possible, avoided. But it could be argued that there is a missed opportunity there. A professor with a lot of research experience and familiarity with libraries may have quite an educated opinion about library services. By providing such an individual a conduit for feedback and being responsive to them, he may be educated about local policies and may provide some suggestions that can innovate services. At the very least, opening up a dialogue will provide an avenue for airing any discontent and hopefully keep him out of the president's office. At most, this person could help make the library better and become a very energetic advocate for the library.

Even individuals within the library who historically have been viewed as detractors or complainers bring a valuable perspective and can have a positive benefit. Listening to a patron who has high expectations that are not met makes the service and the organization improve in an effort to meet his needs; ultimately, that raises the standard and level of service for all.

CHALLENGING THE PROCESS AND RISK TAKING

Kouzes and Posner stated that "all leaders *challenge the process.* Leaders are pioneers—people who are willing to step out into the unknown. They search for opportunities to innovate, grow, and improve."[28] However, have you ever had a leader in the organization that was not willing to step into the unknown and take a risk when they were not 100 percent sure of a positive outcome? Managers who refuse to stick their necks out or challenge anything may do so in fear of being wrong, getting in trouble, or looking stupid. These are the leaders—and once again we use this term loosely—who often throw their team members under the bus when something goes wrong. A service leader, on the other hand, doesn't care about the negative possibilities of risk-taking. They view creativity as a positive characteristic that they often demonstrate when they exhibit unconventional behavior, such as celebrating failure and learning from it. This is not to say that all risk is good. Service leaders recognize that risk-taking must be strategic, weighing the likelihood of success against the repercussions of failure. And if an initiative indeed fails or mistakes are made, it is essential to learn from them.

As stated above, creativity may be drawn from internal vision or external inspiration (or both), but it looks to generate something new and often initiates change. Those who are leading the change are often seen as troublemakers or risk-takers depending on which side of the fence the name-caller is sitting on. According to Rogers, "the most innovative member of a system is very often perceived as a deviant from the social system and is accorded a somewhat status of low credibility by the average members of the system."[29] Roger provides a very telling distinction of a leader's relationship to innovation and to the organization. In many cases, a person might ask, "Is it the titled leadership who has creativity and innovation as a prerogative by virtue of their authority?" We would answer no. It is the person who makes a leader, not the title itself. Inherent in creativity, innovation, and vision is the need to examine and, if necessary, challenge and change the status quo, the standard process, or established norms. By definition this is often seen as being in conflict with the established culture and may be looked on as rebellious, antisocial, or troublemaking. According to Haass, these creative visionaries often "make it your [their] aim to accomplish things, not to avoid criticism."[30] This may be why it is such an uncommon trait in libraries. Roger echoed this statement, saying that "the salient value of the innovator is venturesomeness, due to a desire for the rash, the daring, and the risky. The innovator must also be willing to accept an occasional setback."[31] In other words, risk—the questioning of the status quo, the examination and conjecture on how to improve a process or product, the creation of something entirely new—is practically a requirement for innovation to occur. It is a truism that people fear change. This is why the individuals who do not have positional authority but continue to question the status quo in order to innovate systems are seen as bucking the system and are often considered rabble-rousers or insubordinate. This is why the number-one barrier to creativity and innovation in a library is risk avoidance. This risk avoidance is seen in a number of forms, such as overly complicated processes that act as a barrier to change so that employees do not attempt to examine or change the process in the first place.

Another reason for risk aversion is the reward structure of the organization. Individuals are less likely to takes risks when they are penalized for their mistakes or failures but not rewarded or acknowledged for taking the risk in the first place. Skinner's reinforcement theory describes this dynamic: individuals are punished for risk-taking that results in failure or mistakes, they experience negative reinforcement for doing nothing, and they experience extinction, or a complete lack of acknowledgement for risk-taking with successful outcomes.[32] In the end, this can lead to a stagnating and fearful organization that changes only after it has been tested by other organizations.

The answer is simple: people do not want to be risk-takers because this behavior is often discouraged and they feel that they have something to lose, be it credibility, job security, or respect.

SERVICE LEADERSHIP IN PRACTICE

Jessica sat in a meeting and thought to herself, "I will never get this time back again." As the library was figuring out how to enhance its services, management was repeating the same old mistakes and implementing efforts that they copied from another organization's best practice down the street. Jessica had suggested a couple of pilot projects related to integrating a new service into the eLearning system and had been very excited about the possibility. However, her manager had said that since it had not been implemented anywhere else, there was no way to tell if it would work and they couldn't risk resources on something that might fail.

Jessica sat there asking herself, "Why are we continually speaking about the need to be creative, ground-breaking, and cutting-edge to keep up with the technological changes of today when, push comes to shove, the first thing we do is Google what others are doing and copy it in some way. Why do we do this?"

Like risk-taking, innovation is a value that is inculcated into the organization. It is a way of questioning and learning that not only develops individuals but moves the organization forward. It is a way of thinking strategically.

REFLECTIONS ON INNOVATION: TOOLS FOR DEVELOPMENT

1. What if? When looking at a situation, ask yourself, "what if . . . ?" Thinking about what you would do if there were no boundaries or limitations can help spawn creative ideas. This tactic can be effective in looking for ways to enhance or improve services; it can also be employed to address potential worst-case scenarios and is ideal for emergency planning.
2. Take no out of your vocabulary. When thinking about a possibility or listening to a proposal from someone else, put a hold on the negative response, listen without judging, and ask "why not?" This is a fundamental tenet of excellent service, where no is replaced by a viable alternative or solution.
3. When considering a creative idea, instead of enumerating obstacles and reasons why it is not feasible, ask, "How can we do this?" It leaves the idea on the table, promotes positive discourse, and perpetuates the creative-thinking process as individuals brainstorm solutions.
4. Challenge your preconceptions and patterns. Individuals tend to agree with people who think like they do, so have a conversation with someone you would not regularly seek out. Ask someone out for coffee or, in a regular meeting, sit where you would not normally sit; it will give you a different perspective and could get you out of a rut. While simple, it can change the entire dynamic.
5. Challenge the status quo. This could take a very structured form in terms of regularly reviewing policy and procedures and promoting discussion about how they could be improved. It could also be spontaneous, but there are some times when it is more effective or more appropriate to do this than others.
6. Value the rabble-rouser. Individuals, whether patrons or employees, may make unpopular suggestions through complaints or through an effort to make positive change. While strong negative emotion is something that most people try to avoid, it can be an opportunity to hear an unpopular (but not necessarily wrong or misguided) viewpoint. An employee or patron may be more than disgruntled; she could be the canary in the coal mine, offering feedback about something that

could be improved. In addition, if someone is that passionate about an issue, it is possible to engage them and redirect that energy to a positive solution.

7. Have you ever attended a large meeting in which you were asking a question for clarification and your boss told you loudly to be quiet? How did it make you feel? What was the general feeling in the room as this happened? Did you feel motivated to ask additional questions or to even care about the outcome of the meeting? Now imagine if you were a boss. Do you believe you have the same working relationship with your employee as you did before you told him/her to be quiet?

8. Now, as a boss, imagine if the question that your employee was asking was critical to the success of your project and you simply didn't know because you didn't listen or understand. Imagine how the rest of the room might view your actions. Imagine the implications for the success of the project.

NOTES

1. Walt Disney, as quoted in the ending credits of *Meet the Robinsons* (2007) www.brainyquote.com/quotes/quotes/w/waltdisney132637.html.

2. Lessons from Walt Disney, The McManigle Company, http://mcmanigle.com/uncategorized/lessons-walt-disney.

3. Svafa Grönfeldt and Judith Strother, *Service Leadership: The Quest for Competitive Advantage* (Thousand Oaks, CA: Sage Publications, 2006), 135.

4. Bill Leban and Romuald Stone, *Managing Organizational Change,* 2nd ed. (Hoboken, NJ: John Wiley, 2008), 155.

5. Montgomery Van Wart, *Dynamics of Leadership in Public Service: Theory and Practice,* 2nd ed. (Armonk, New York: M.E. Sharpe, 2011), 212.

6. Richard Hughes, Robert Ginnett, and Gordon Curphy, *Leadership: Enhancing the Lessons of Experience,* 3rd ed. (Boston, MA: Irwin McGraw Hill, 1999), 249–250.

7. Ibid., 251.

8. Barbara I. Dewey, "Public Services Librarians in the Academic Community: The Imperative for Leadership," in *Leadership and Academic Librarians,* eds. Terrence F. Mech and Gerard B. McCabe (Westport, CT: Greenwood Press, 1998), 92.

9. Frank Lewis Dyer and Thomas Commerford Martin, "Edison: His Life and Inventions" (Hyperion Works, 2014). Downloaded from Project Gutenberg.

10. Peter M. Senge, *The Fifth Discipline: The Art & Practice of the Learning Organization* (New York, NY: Doubleday, 1990); Dusya Vera and Mary Crossan, "Strategic Leadership and Organizational Learning," *The Academy of Management Review* 29, no. 2 (2004): 222–240.

11. Richard N. Haass, *The Bureaucratic Entrepreneur: How to be Effective in Any Unruly Organization* (Washington, DC: Brookings Institution, 1999), 46.

12. Peter M. Senge, *The Fifth Discipline: The Art & Practice of the Learning Organization* (New York, NY: Doubleday, 1990), 208.

13. Gary Yukl, *Leadership in Organizations*, 6th ed. (Upper Saddle River, NJ: Prentice Hall, 2006), 268

14. Robert F. Russell and A. Gregory Stone, "A Review of Servant Leadership Attributes: Developing a Practice Model," *Leadership and Organization Development Journal* 23, no. 3 (2002): 147.

15. Leon C. Megginson, "Lessons from Europe for American Business," *Southwestern Social Science Quarterly* 44, no. 1 (1963): 4.

16. Beth A. Hennessy and Terisa M. Amabile, "Conditions of Creativity" in *The Nature of Creativity: Contemporary Psychological Perspectives*, ed. Robert J. Sternberg (New York, NY: Cambridge University Press, 1988): 11–38.

17. Richard Hughes, Robert Ginnett, and Gordon Curphy, *Leadership: Enhancing the Lessons of Experience*, 5th ed. (Boston, MA: Irwin McGraw Hill, 1999), 181.

18. Donald E. Riggs, "The Crisis and Opportunities in Library Leadership," in *Leadership in the Library and Information Science Professions: Theory and Practice*, ed. Mark D. Winston (New York, NY: Haworth, 2001), 11.

19. Ibid., 16.

20. Svafa Grönfeldt and Judith Strother, *Service Leadership: The Quest for Competitive Advantage* (Thousand Oaks, CA: Sage Publications, 2006), 137.

21. Ibid., 137–138.

22. Gifford Pinchot, *Intrapreneuring* (New York, NY: Harper & Row, 1985), 22.

23. Svafa Grönfeldt and Judith Strother, *Service Leadership: The Quest for Competitive Advantage* (Thousand Oaks, CA: Sage Publications, 2006), 134–135.

24. Bill Leban and Romuald Stone, *Managing Organizational Change,* 2nd ed. (Hoboken, NJ: John Wiley, 2008), 6.

25. Ibid.

26. Christoph Lueneburger, *A Culture of Purpose: How to Choose the Right People and Make the Right People Choose You* (San Francisco, CA: Jossey-Bass, 2014), 19–20.

27. Christine M. Pearson and Judith A. Clair, "Reframing Crisis Management," *The Academy of Management Review* 23 no. 1 (1998): 60.

28. James M. Kouzes and Barry Z. Posner, *The Leadership Challenge*, 3rd ed. (San Francisco, CA: Jossey-Bass, 2002), 17.

29. Everett M. Rogers, *Diffusion of Innovations*, 5th ed. (New York, NY: Free Press, 2003), 26.

30. Richard N. Haass, *The Bureaucratic Entrepreneur: How to be Effective in Any Unruly Organization* (Washington, DC: Brookings Institution, 1999): 38.

31. Everett M. Rogers, *Diffusion of Innovations*, 5th ed. (New York, NY: Free Press, 2003), 283.

32. B.F. Skinner, *Science and Human Behavior* (New York, NY: Free Press, 1953).

CHAPTER 7

··

STRATEGIC PLANNING

··

The Practice of Innovation and Strategic Thinking

Strategy without process is little more than a wish list.
—*Robert Filek*[1]

W hen people in large organizations hear the words *strategic plan*, there is likely a collective groan. Many have a strategic planning process, with an emphasis on process. A strategic plan is intended to be concrete so that everyone in the organization has a map to follow. The plan is meaningless if it does not inform the priorities or actions of the organization. But since it is immutable and because it is usually approved or directed from the top, it is difficult to change or to adapt; and it is almost impossible to be agile from the front lines.

Strategy, on the other hand, is less about planning and more about a way of thinking or engaging with the environment. Strategic thinking is embedded in the culture; it manifests intentionally in strategic-planning activities. Strategic planning is the concrete manifestation of innovation, a way for the organization to evolve and develop in view of a big picture.

Related to strategic thinking and critical to the process of strategic planning is the concept of systems thinking. This is the acknowledgement that many factors influence a situation, similar to an ecosystem where plants, animals, the weather, geology, and many other details all influence each other. This is a fundamental principle with regard to strategic planning because it means that solutions are complex and results may be unforeseen. Senge discusses the systems-thinking model and postulates eleven laws that provide a helpful framework:

1. "Today's problems come from yesterday's solutions...
2. The harder you push, the harder the system pushes back...
3. Behavior grows better before it grows worse...
4. The easy way out usually leads back in...
5. The cure can be worse than the disease...
6. Faster is slower...

7. Cause and effect are not closely related in time and space…
8. Small changes can produce big results—but the areas of highest leverage are often the least obvious…
9. You can have your cake and eat it too—but not at once…
10. Dividing an elephant in half does not produce two small elephants…
11. There is no blame."[2]

While his laws are rather pithy, Senge's points are highly relevant to the strategic-planning process and uncover some issues that are largely overlooked and impact the success of the plan and its outcomes.

Despite Filek's warning, which has been echoed by many leaders over the years, creating a strategy without creating a plan is exactly what a lot of organizations do. How many times have you sat in what seems like the same strategic planning meeting and heard the same old lines:

- What is the library's mission?
- What are our values?
- Where do we want to be in 10 years?
- How do we get there?
- What is working and what isn't?

Once the meeting (or possibly even a more lengthy retreat) is over, nothing is really accomplished beyond what was said in the meeting, with the exception of scheduling another meeting next year to repeat the same process. No decisions are made, no data gathered or evidence presented, no goals fixed or timeline set. The meeting is attended by a group of managers and colleagues who may be so far removed from the library's service points that they are guessing at the answers. The strategic planning meeting seems so scripted and repetitive that it would almost be sufficient to record it once and rewatch it the next year. Far too often leaders are confused about what a strategic plan is and spend little, if any, time thinking about the plan's process and implementation. Service leaders know that in order to think ahead they need to look back.[3] This goes beyond thinking about how to progress from where an organization currently is to determining what the future state or desirable conclusion is and what the steps are to get there. This big picture thinking is not meant to advocate a Machiavellian perspective but rather to assert that the actions in the interim should align with the end in mind and that they should also be consistent with personal and organizational service-oriented values. That said, the idea that it is the journey, not the destination is also not desirable. With a focus on the process, nothing gets accomplished, as exemplified by committees that meet regularly but never have any outcomes or impact.

Also of significance, employees hate to feel that their time was wasted, which can be perceived as a lack of respect. Engaging employees on a plan to move the organization forward but neglecting to follow through and implement the plan may create perception on the part of employees that the plan was not worthy of implementation and engender feelings of distrust and resentment toward the leader. This is another example of saying one thing and doing something else.

However, following through also reaches beyond strategic planning, encompassing not only the decision that the leader makes but relating it to the values that she promotes. For example, if a leader claims that everyone should feel comfortable to try new things and take risks, she must stand by this risk-taking behavior, creating a safe environment for employees to take risks and fail. Conger and Kanungo, for example, believe that during the implementation stage of change, charismatic leaders rely on "unconventional means and exhibit behaviors of self-sacrifice and personal risk-taking to align commitment from followers and to empower them to act."[4]

What service leaders realize, in terms of sustainability, is that good intentions (or in the meeting case below, words) mean nothing; it is actions that will move their organization forward, and these actions are achieved through the develop-

SERVICE LEADERSHIP IN PRACTICE

Strategic planning can bring out the worst in organizations and individuals. For example, a university library has recently hired a new director, Evan, and he put in place a management team by virtue of hires through searches, hiring individuals from his previous institution, and promoting internal candidates. As with all new administrations, there is a concerted effort to redefine the priorities in view of the new leadership—essentially, remake the organization in their image. For purposes of inclusion, it was decided that a strategic planning retreat, including the heads of all the units, would jump-start these efforts. The venue was set outside of the library to put people at ease, and each unit head was instructed to bring ideas, issues, and concerns that they had gathered from their units. At the retreat, they broke up into round tables to address overarching topics; the effort was to identify the major areas of focus through discussion and consensus. Instead, what occurred was a lot of posturing and protection of sacred cows, with unit heads pushing their own agenda and ignoring the big picture. Because of the competing agenda and lack of vision, there are no action items and no outcomes. But in six months, another retreat will be scheduled.

ment and implementation of a strategic plan. Service leaders know that "strategy is about selection of goals and objectives, which is what makes every single strategy unique in nature."[5] A strategic plan is not a document used solely to trot out to upper administration when the dean's supervisor wants to see it. A strategic plan is a guiding force that signals to the individuals in the organization what direction they should be heading. This is why strategic plans must be regularly reviewed, evaluated, and updated to address the ever-changing environment. Drucker supports this continual review when he states, "strategic planning is the continuous process of making present entrepreneurial risk-taking *decisions* systematically and with the greatest knowledge of their futurity; organizing systematically the *efforts* needed to carry out these decisions; and measuring the results of these decisions against the expectations through organized, *systematic feedback*."[6] Each of these elements is critical and dependent on the other: planning, implementation, and assessment, which then feeds back into the planning process.

Libraries, like many organizations, use strategic planning as a technique to plan today where they want to be in the future. However, before a library can plan where it wants to be, it needs to assess where it is and how it got to where it currently is. The plan, or strategic plan as it is called in the business world, is the document that communicates to the library employees what the library's goals are and what actions the library as a whole needs to take so that it can achieve these goals. Strategic planning is one management activity that libraries can use like a Global Positioning System (GPS) to lead them to where they want to be and to help a library know what actions to make to achieve its vision as well as when the library is ultimately successful in achieving its goal. In short, a strategic plan will help a service leader and her library team set their priorities in order to strengthen the library's operations, and it also will help identify where and how the library should focus its energy and resources so that all the library employees are working toward a common library vision. According to Riggs, "Unlike traditional planning, which normally results in a neatly bound document collecting dust on a shelf, strategic planning is more dynamic with annual updates and primary emphasis on strategies (courses of action designed to achieve goals and objectives)."[7] Consequently, as stated above, a strategic plan is a never-finished document because the plan is always evolving and the strategic-planning process never ending. A service leader recognizes this and must be willing to adjust the organization's strategic plan in response to the changing environment in order to include new ideas to strengthen the library's operations.

THE ATTRIBUTES OF A STRATEGIC PLAN

The first step of a strategic-planning process relates to gathering intelligence to help shape the direction of the process. Organizations should generally look at doing a needs assessment of their primary clientele; in the case of libraries, this may be a survey, focus groups, or another type of information gathering about their patrons. It is an essential step for service-driven organizations.

Although the features that make up a strategic plan vary depending on the organization, according to Riggs there are nine common attributes that help to frame most strategic plans. These nine elements are: vision statement, mission statement, goals, objectives, strategy and timeline, responsibility, explanation of work, resource allocation, and assessment.[8]

A vision statement tells not only the organization's employees but also its stakeholders what and where the library wants to be in the future. Vision statements should be general and are a declaration of the library's key goals for the midterm and long-term future. However, since the library's environment is changing so rapidly due to the technological advancements, library administrators should not try to project beyond 10 years in the organization's future. Vision statements can range from one line to several pages and provide the employees with more than just what the library would like to achieve or accomplish; they also provide an inspiration for the day-to-day operations of a library and are used to mold the library's strategic decisions. Vision statements help to unify all employees to achieve a common goal so that they can be more productive. This is an example of a vision statement from the Alzheimer's Association: "Our vision is a world without Alzheimer's."[9]

Unlike vision statements, mission statements are a brief but succinct statement that defines the present state or purpose of the library for its employees and stakeholders. Mission statements generally answer three common questions about why the library exists and what it focuses on:

- What does the library do?
- What community does it serve?
- How does the library do what it does?

Most academic libraries, for example, generally state in their mission statements that they support and aid the academic institution's curriculum, instruction, and research mission.

Goals and objectives quite often are used interchangeably, but they are not synonymous. Goals build on both the vision and mission statements by bringing a sense of order and priority to the library's actions. They are written down and clearly specify the library's purpose. Goals give the library administration and its employees a sense of a long-term direction by specifying in detail the library's long-range priorities. One important point to make is that goals are not ideals. It would seem strange, for instance, for an academic library to create a goal that says it wants to develop the most prestigious music collection in a specific state when it doesn't have a music department. This goal is even more unrealistic and unattainable because the library is facing cuts to its acquisitions budget. Goals must be attainable and specific enough so that they can be converted into measurable objectives. Objectives are short-term intentions that need to be clearly stated, measurable, and verifiable. Objectives are commonly written in relation to a specific result with an assigned date of completion so that the library can point to these completed objectives as landmarks in achieving their overarching goals.

Strategy, within the context of an articulated plan, is the meat of all strategic plans because it is where the library specifies how it will achieve its goals and objectives. It is in the strategy section of the plan where the steps to implementing the strategic plan are spelled out. This section identifies who will do what and how they will do it. This is where the rubber hits the road. Service leaders know that one strategy is not a one-glove-fits-all type of situation and as a result generates different strategies for each goal and objective the library wishes to achieve.

Timelines are critical when carrying out strategies. Without specifying how long it should take to complete a specific task, library administrators can create problems and affect the possibility of the strategy being achieved. Those responsible for completing the task can view the lack of timeline as a lack of importance to the organization and consequently put off attempting to work on the task because they believe it is not a high priority. However, when a timeline is attached to a specific project completion, team members see that the organization values the task and work toward completing it. However, it is important to remember that when setting a timeline to carry out the task that the time allotted needs to be reasonable and doable. Take, for example, a staff member assigned a goal of recataloging all two million AACRII records in their catalog to RDA records in one month. This goal is completely unreasonable and cannot be accomplished in the allotted time period. Setting such an unreasonable time frame not only will anger your team members but will also create a sense of distrust in the leader's understanding of what the team does. Employees believe that the leader should have known that it was impossible to accomplish such a mammoth task in such a short time frame.

Having consistent, clear, and agreed-upon expectations of job responsibility is important to ensure that library employees are not overcommitted and don't become overwhelmed when trying to complete one or more strategies in a brief time. As stated above, realistic timelines help with limiting this feeling of overcommitment, but understanding an employee's workload is also critical. Libraries struggle with understanding and defining workload, particularly for librarians since all too often we ourselves cannot define what we do. Adding to this issue revolves around the saying: "if you want something done, ask a busy person."[10] There is a lot of truth in this statement, which is generally attributed to Benjamin Franklin, since the busier a person is, the better that person has learned to manage his time. However, continually giving a busy person more work assignments can cause employee burnout and create resentment as the employee looks around at the people who seem to be doing less and often spending most of their time gossiping around the water cooler or counting down the minutes until it the five o'clock whistle. This resentment may increase when a part-time leadership opportunity in another department arises, such as an interim associate dean of faculties' position, but her team leader is unable to define what her workload is and so, the departments could not agree on what part-time looked like and the time commitment. As a result, the opportunity vanishes, leaving the employee upset and disillusioned with the organization.

Resources required to accomplish the strategic plan relate to the assets a library has to use when implementing its strategic plan. Resources can be human capital, equipment, finances, and even information technology. To accomplish any task, resources must be identified, committed, and allocated to get the job done. Far too often, library administration underestimates what it will take to accomplish a specific task. The fact that library administration is often farther removed from the actual day-to-day running of the organization results in a lack of true understanding of their team's workload and processes in the organization. Leaders who don't discuss with their teams what is needed to implement the strategic plan can underestimate what it takes, resulting in a failed implementation.

Annually, assessments occur when the service leader looks back at all she and her team have done to achieve the library's goals in order to identify what worked and what didn't. It is a time when the objectives that were achieved are removed from the plan and new objectives added. Where strategies failed, the service leader identifies another strategy that she feels might work better, basing it on the information that has come to light while reassessing the plan. However, there should also be checkpoints at different stages of a project or initiative; this allows the ability to evaluate whether efforts are on track, make course corrections if needed, or adapt if circumstances have changed.

Now that we have examined the nuts and bolts of a strategic plan and have clarified the basic terms, such as vision, mission, objectives, and goals, and how they relate to the organization as a whole, we will take a look at the strategic plan design and how it is developed.

DESIGNING THE STRATEGIC PLAN

Developing any strategic plan is a complex process, particularly for those institutions, such as libraries, where change is constant and fear of the outcome of this change brings out distrust and suspicion in some people. To aid in relieving this suspicion, service leaders may take the step and "listen to themselves" in order to become aware of their biases and listen to their employees to be aware of the work environment. By doing this service leaders are helping to address this distrust; however, no matter what steps a service leader takes, there will always be a small number of people who are going to be resistant to the change. The key for a service leader is to understand the reason for this resistance. One very basic reason harkens back to the discussion in chapter 3 discussing trust or, more specifically, the lack of trust. After all, don't we always say that in order to avoid mistakes in the future we must learn from the past? Well, if the employee was burned in the past, wouldn't she learn from this experience and avoid it in the future? Perhaps it was Joseph Heller, author of *Catch 22*, who said it best: "Just because you're paranoid doesn't mean they aren't after you." This statement has become one that people live by. But in order to break the cycle of mistrust and create an environment open to change and innovation, a transparent strategic-planning process must be developed hand-in-hand with those affected by the future change.

A simple literature search on *strategic planning process models* or *strategic plan design* brings to light the plethora of articles describing the many different strategic-planning process models and the importance of transparency to the process. The reason for this, particularly for libraries, is that the fast pace of technological change within the profession has made it challenging for service leaders to anticipate what may be coming and position the library in a way to meet this change. As it became apparent that web technology was transforming libraries and would continue to do so, the buzz word at the beginning of the 1990s was *agile*. By the latter half of the 1990s and into the 2000s, the idea of being agile was scoffed at, and strategic planning was largely dismissed as unrealistic due to the need to be responsive to the rapidly changing environment, particularly for large libraries. Despite this dismissive behavior toward strategic planning, there were a number of academic library leaders who recognized the need to redefine their role on campus so that the library and its services would become more relevant to its users. For example, Stoffle et al. stressed this need, stating, "The choice is clear. Change now and choose our futures. Change later, or not at all, and have no future."[11]

The reason for this shift in attitude was largely due both to internal and external drivers. Some internal drivers included shrinking budgets, new initiatives, and service improvement efforts. External drivers included the proliferation of technology, increasing patron demand, increased calls for accountability and assessment, and other economic concerns, such as serials inflation. Even generational issues among employees had and continue to have a profound impact on libraries in terms of employees' and supervisors' expectations, particularly around human resource practices related to job performance expectations, evaluation, and rewards. As a result librarians are seeing an increase in the use of strategic-planning models such as environmental scans, an exercise that examines the factors that may impact an organization or effort. Environmental scans can take various forms, the most common being: strengths, weaknesses, opportunities, and threats (SWOT) analysis; and STEP Diagrams to help develop a library strategic plan. The STEP analysis or diagram was originally developed by Francis J. Aguilar to provide a lens for developing an environmental scan, specifically in terms of economic, social, technological, and political factors. This model has evolved over time to incorporate various other aspects, the most common being legal and security.[12]

SWOT, which will be discussed in detail below, was developed in the 1960s by Albert Humphrey to help identify and evaluate the strengths, weaknesses, opportunities, and threats facing a business, including the services a business offers and the people who deliver and receive those services. STEP diagrams, on the other hand, are designed by library administration to illustrate the string of progressive steps necessary to carry out a specific work process or procedure. However, as you can see from figure 7.1, most of these different models have a number of similar qualities, or process steps, that walk a service leader through the strategic-planning process. The model used in this chapter is adapted from Morgenstern and Jones's Strategic Planning Process model but has been altered to reflect the servant leader's approach to the strategic-planning process.[13] There are nine steps, spelled out below, that may be overlooked since leaders often skip steps and jump into the SWOT analysis part of the model, without having an accurate and thorough understanding of the importance of listening during the gathering-data steps.[14] In addition, some leaders completely put aside the vision statement of the library, attempting to implement a strategic plan without thinking about where the organization wants to be in the future.

CRISIS MANAGEMENT

When an organization is facing a crisis, such as when there is a surprising negative event or unforeseen consequence of an event which could threaten an organization, it requires a service leader to be innovative and make a quick decision to minimize the damage of the event. Pearson and Clair believe that "Organizational crisis management is a systematic attempt by organizational members with external stakeholders to avert crises or to effectively manage those that do occur. Organizational crisis management effectiveness is evidenced when potential crises are averted or when key stakeholders believe that the success outcomes of short- and long-range impacts of crises outweigh the failure outcomes."[15]

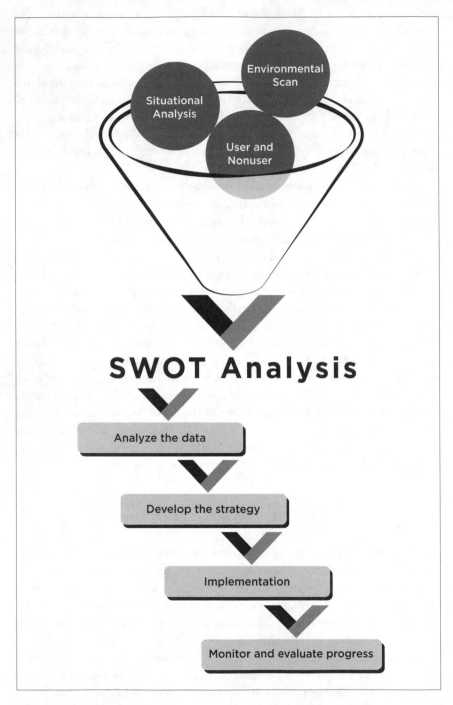

Figure 7.1 SWOT Analysis

SITUATION ANALYSIS, ENVIRNOMENTAL SCAN, AND USER/NONUSERS SCAN

Situation analysis is the first step of the strategic planning process as the service leader starts reviewing the library's mission statement and then begins the process of gathering data from all of its stakeholders, including its employees and patrons, in view of this mission statement. This is important because service leaders need to analyze and understand their library's own current state and environment, and this is done in three different stages: situation analaysis, environmental scan, and user/nonuser scan. These three data-gathering steps are critical for performing the SWOT analysis. The first data-gathering step is situation analysis, which deals with the library's internal environment. The results of this analysis should highlight the library's internal strengths and weaknesses. This analysis is where a service leader discovers which library services are *actually* working and which are not. Historically, leaders make the mistake of rushing to the SWOT analaysis first, assuming that they know what is working and what is not working in their library. However, as discussed in chapter 3 on Conscientiousness and chapter 4 on Building Rapport, the service leader does not assume anything and listens to those around her. Often it is hard to hear what your library's weakness is, and some leaders prefer to ignore this information, chalking it up to the opinion of disgruntled employees. Nevertheless, it is critical to listen objectively to those around you.

The second data-gathering step is the environmental scan stage. This is the part of the data-gathering process that looks at the library's external environment. It is this step that describes the opportunities and threats to the organization, the *OT* in SWOT. The threats identify what will undermine a library service if it is not addressed through change. It is during this stage that possible competitors of the library are also identified. Opportunities, on the other hand, highlight what the library can do to take advantage of the changing environment in order to improve or develop a potential service. According to Morgenstern and Jones, many strategic plans fail because the external environment step of the planning process is not deep or critical enough because it is poorly executed and often rooted in the present and the familiar while not probing enough into the future possiblities.[16]

The third step in the data-collection stage involves the library's users and nonusers. Specifically, the library must examine usage and behavior patterns as well as users' perceptions of the library and the services it offers. Often libraries struggle with gathering this information because they find it difficult to understand why their services are not used. It is hard for any librarian to hear students say that libraries are irrelevant and Google has everything, which of course it doesn't.

Once all this critical information is gathered, the library leader can begin to analyze the data objectivly using a strategic-planning tool, such as SWOT. It is here that one places all the information together and begins asking the strategic questions. However, if the library leaders ignore the critical data-gathering steps because they assume they know this information and consequenlty move directly into the SWOT analysis, the SWOT analysis will fail because the data used in it will be corrupt and biased by the leaders' perception.

STRENGTHS, WEAKNESSES, OPPORTUNITIES, AND THREATS (SWOT)

Using the data gathered during the first three stages of the strategic planning process, the service leader begins the fourth stage, the SWOT analysis. This analysis tool has become one of the most widely used strategic planning tools and can be used by service leaders to look at their library and its services objectively. As the service leader plots the data gathered during the first three phases of the stragetic planning model, he will be able to see an action plan. Below is an example of a completed SWOT analysis.

Generally, it is presented in a grid, with strengths opposite weaknesses, describing the aspects internal to the organizations, as illustrated in the example below:

Strengths

1. Staff and faculty are stable, committed, diverse, and educated
2. Library building is centrally located
3. Library has a comprehensive collection of both print and online material
4. Space is attractive and inviting
5. Coffee shop makes library inviting
6. Library has a strong interlibrary loan department

Weaknesses

1. Lack of managerial depth and talent
2. Plagued with internal operating problems
3. Space is tight and has few outlets for computers
4. Inventory system needs to be updated
5. Weak leaders with poor communication skills
6. Organizational culture is fragmented, causing a decrease in staff and faculty motivation and support for the library

7. Relative to other libraries of the same size, staffing numbers are too low to support current services
8. Lack of specialized personnel
9. Outdated organizational structure
10. Lack of service-level agreements
11. Funding cuts have forced library to reduce its purchase of foreign language materials

Opportunities and threats are usually presented in the bottom half of the grid to indicate the external environmental factors that should be considered in doing an environmental scan.

Opportunities

1. Increase wireless access in library
2. Create additional opportunities for library programming and services
3. Increase usage of cloud computing
4. Diversify services
5. Promote open access
6. Build storage facility to allow library to alleviate stack space to increase users space
7. Purchase new inventory system

Threats

1. Changing patron base
2. Technological advances
3. Unfocused message of library vision and mission
4. Poor communication has created an active grapevine that passes gossip
5. Lack of priorities
6. Hostile security environment
7. Decrease in library funding
8. User's impression that the library is obsolete
9. Strategic planning at the university level does not involve the library in the process
10. Increased cost for electronic books and journals

When filling out the SWOT grid it is important to note that strengths and weaknesses are often internal factors to your library, while opportunities and threats are often related to external factors. The word *often* is used in the previous sentence because service leaders recognize that they must consider their library's strengths and weaknesses both from an internal perspective and from the library's patron's point of view. In addition, the opportunities and threats do not always come from external factors but could come from within the library itself, such as disgruntled employees and poor library management.

When assessing a library's strengths and weaknesses, a service leader looks at the data collected and places it in the context of the library's users' needs not just of the library's needs. It is necessary to ask questions like: what does the library do well and where is it falling short of its mission? Service leaders achieve this understanding by constantly considering both the view of the library and the view of its patrons as they fill out the strengths and weakness section of the analysis. While filling out the strength section, service leaders need to be realistic and truthful. Once completed, the grid should state what the library's advantages are and what it does well. Often the strengths section seems easy to fill out because it is easy to identify what your team is doing well. Weaknesses, however, are not so easy to identify because people tend to gloss over their weaknesses or, worse, avoid identifying them because they either don't know what they are doing wrong or don't want to know. When incorrectly identifying weaknesses, the library only perpetuates the problems and further damages the organization. The weaknesses section should answer the questions: How can the library improve? What are we not doing well? What should we stop doing?

All too often leaders get lost in the first two sections of a SWOT analysis and never get to the opportunities and threats sections of the model. This lack of attention to the external environment causes the library to be less effective in delivering valuable services to its patrons: the positive event may create an opportunity to enhance service or improves processes that are overlooked; the negative event may pose a threat that is unanticipated and might disrupt valuable services for its patrons.[17] When trying to identify your library's opportunities, examine your strengths to see if they open up any opportunities and also look at your weaknesses to see if eliminating the weakness will open up an opportunity for the library. Service leaders ask themselves questions such as: What are possible opportunities for the library and what are interesting trends we see in the library science field? Libraries have experienced a lot of change in the past couple of decades, and it only seems to be accelerating. Due to new technology, the evolving political and economic climate, and demands for increasing accountability from decision-makers and users alike, change has become the one constant. This makes it much more difficult to anticipate what the future will hold and therefore makes it challenging to plan long-term initiatives. However, it is the responsibility of the service leader to make these efforts and help create a plan that is adaptable to change. In spite of that, it is not uncommon to hear an administrator laugh at the concept of planning for the future because there is just too much change.

While it is true that there is change, this attitude neither inspires confidence nor provides guidance for growth.

The fourth section of a SWOT analysis is threats. This section focuses on the external factors that are beyond the library's control and place the library and its services at risk. Take for example the establishment of the internet; it was believed that the internet would be the end of libraries since all items, it was believed, would be available on the internet. Was it truly the end of libraries, or did it just change the way libraries deliver their services? Although libraries have no control over these types of external threats, it is important for service leaders to have strategic plans to address them and to use them as a possible opportunity. To help identify threats to library service, leaders can pose questions such as these: What obstacles does the library currently face and what are the possible obstacles in the future? Which other libraries and information service companies are our competitors? How is technology threatening or helping the library? Can any of the library's weaknesses seriously threaten it or can they be used as an opportunity?

DEVELOPING STRATEGIES

Once the SWOT analysis is completed, the service leader begins the process of reviewing the data and developing both short- and long term strategies to maximize the library's strengths while minimizing its weaknesses. This is achieved by examining how the library's strengths, weaknesses, opportunities, and threats might inform one another and utilizing these intersections to come up with ways to help the organization. This is done by asking the following questions:

1. Which of the library's strengths identified in the SWOT analysis can be used to maximize the opportunities identified?
2. How can the library's strengths identified in the SWOT analysis be used to minimize the threats identified?
3. What actions can be taken to minimize the library's weaknesses identified in the SWOT analysis by using the opportunities identified?
4 How can the library's weaknesses identified in the SWOT analysis be minimized to avoid the threats identified?

Take, for example, the list of strengths identified in the sample completed SWOT Analysis grid. Can any of those strengths be used to maximize the items listed under the library's opportunities? Can those strengths also be used to minimize the threats identified in the analysis? A service leader would next look at the opportunities identified in the SWOT analysis to help develop strategies that minimize the weaknesses that have the possibility of becoming future threats.

After completing this step, the service leader will be able not only to identify and define the strategies the library will use to move forward but also to spell out more clearly the library's vision, its short- and long-term objectives, the goals to achieve specific objectives, and its implementation plan to achieve its goals. Once the plan is implemented and goals are met, it is important to remember to review the progress of the strategic plan in order to assess its successes and failures and to adjust the plan where necessary.

ASSESSING THE LIBRARY'S STRATEGIC PLAN

Historically, far too often library administrators have skipped over the assessment of their library's strategic plan, thinking that since they followed an organized process, the plan is successful. Not so. Assessment and accountability are not just a couple of buzzwords used by academic administration in order to appease those who pay the bills. It is a critical step in discovering if the library is moving in the right direction to fulfill its mission and reach its vision. Although examined in more detail in chapter 9, assessment as it relates to strategic planning needs to be briefly considered below.

As stated above, all too often assessment is an afterthought in the strategic planning process, something that is tacked on at the end of the process or effort. This is problematic for a number of reasons; these are the two most significant:

- Without some sort of continuous monitoring or evaluation, there is no way to make a mid-course correction due to new events or unantici- pated results.
- If assessment is not a fundamental assumption and an integral part of the strategic planning process, then it is unlikely that the library admin- istrator will know if the strategic plan is working.

In order to avoid skipping the assessment step of the strategic planning process, service leaders can utilize assessment models. One such model is the ADDIE model, named for the steps involved: analyze, design, develop, implement, evalu- ate. ADDIE is a learning theory model that came out of the military; its core assumes a repetitive approach to assessment as it relates to projects and strategic planning.[18] Each step of the ADDIE model advocates a review or assessment check, even prior to the overall program or project evaluation. This establishes that the criteria for evaluation are relevant and rest on informed decisions.

In libraries it is not uncommon for the criteria for evaluation to be based on metrics that are easily available, but these metrics may not be as relevant for the decision-making process. For example, what does the number of books cataloged in a library say about the activity of the library? While it does describe activity within one area, it may not be representative of service demand, usage, or even quality of performance. However, libraries may report those metrics because they are relatively uncomplicated and easily obtained. Obtaining significant and representative data takes planning and should be a fundamental part of the strategic planning process. Assessment data also needs to be tied to the plan's strategic goals so that this data can inform the success of those efforts or indicate changes that may need to be made.

The initial analysis or mid-term evaluation is also valuable in terms of budgeting or resource allocation, staffing, and organizational structure. It can help answer concerns about whether there are enough and/or the appropriate resources for the effort to succeed. The assessment might even help to indicate whether it is worth the expenditure of effort to continue.

REFLECTIONS ON STRATEGIC PLANNING: TOOLS FOR DEVELOPMENT

1. Think about your mission (either at an individual or unit level). Who are your patrons? What are their needs? And how do those answers inform the mission?
2. Draft a SWOT.
3. List your library's strongest attributes.
   a. List the things your library does that no other library or company does.
   b. List what your library patrons like best about your library and its services.
   c. List the areas of your library where you are facing fiscal constraints and where these constraints are affecting performance.
   d. List other areas that need improvement.
   e. List what your library patrons would like to see changed in the library.
   f. List all the things your library could do if it had the proper funding.
   g. List all the things your library could do if it took advantage of current technologies and advancements.
   h. List how your strengths could help achieve the opportunities listed above.
   i. List what could be and what currently is negatively impacting your library.
   j. List what library services are being offered to your library patrons by other companies or institutions.

     k. List what could, in the future, or what currently is creating a weakness in your library that may make you at risk for future funding cuts.[19]

4. A classic question to ask is: Where do you want the organization to be in five years (or 10 or . . .)? This provides the general direction for the organization (or individual) and allows the creation of milestones to achieve this vision.

5. Think of a project in which you have been involved. Was there a time in that project when a mid-term evaluation or milestone check would ultimately have made it more successful?

NOTES

1. "10 Quotes About Strategy," http://sweetmanager.blogspot.com/2013/05/10-quotes-about-strategy.html.
2. Peter M. Senge and Joel Suzuki, *The Fifth Discipline: The Art and Practice of the Learning Organization* (New York, NY: Currency Doubleday, 1994), 57–67.
3. Richard N. Haass, *The Bureaucratic Entrepreneur: How to be Effective in Any Unruly Organization* (Washington D.C.: Brookings Institution, 1999), 46.
4. Jay A. Conger, Rabindra N. Kanungo, Sanjay T. Menon, and Purnima Mathur, "Measuring Charisma: Dimensionality and Validity of the Conger-Kanungo Scale of Charismatic Leadership," *Canadian Journal of Administrative Sciences* 14, no. 3 (2009): 291.
5. Svafa Grönfeldt and Judith Strother, *Service Leadership: The Quest for Competitive Advantage* (Thousand Oaks, CA: Sage Publications, 2006), 96.
6. Peter R. Drucker, *Management Tasks, Responsibilities, Practices* (Oxford: Butterworth Hienemann, 1974), 120.
7. Donald E. Riggs, "Visionary Leadership," in *Leadership and Academic Libraries,* eds. Terrence F. Mech and Gerard B. McCabe (Westport CT: Greenwood Press, 1998), 58.
8. Ibid., 59–60.
9. Alzheimer's Association website, www.alz.org.
10. Jerome Agel and Walter D. Glanze, *Pearls of Wisdom: A Harvest of Quotations from All Ages* (New York, NY: Harper Row, 1987), 6.
11. Carla Stoffle, Robert Renaud, and Jerilyn R. Veldof, "Choosing our Futures," *College & Research Libraries* 57, no. 3 (May 1996): 224.
12. Francis Joseph Aguilar, *Scanning the Business Environment* (New York, NY: Macmillan, 1967).
13. Jim Morgenstern and Rebecca Jones, "Library Strategic Planning: Voyage of Starship Enterprise or Spruce Goose?" *Feliciter* 58, no. 5 (October 2012):12–14.
14. Ibid.
15. Christine M. Pearson and Judith A. Clair, "Reframing Crisis Management," *The Academy of Management Review* 23, no. 1 (1998): 61.
16. Jim Morgenstern and Rebecca Jones, "Library Strategic Planning: Voyage of Starship Enterprise or Spruce Goose?" *Feliciter* 58, no. 5 (October 2012): 12–14.

17. O. Ferrell, M. Hartline, G. Lucas, D. Luck, *Marketing Strategy* (Orlando, FL: Dryden Press, 1998).

18. Robert K. Branson et al., *Interservice Procedures for Instructional Systems Development. Executive Summary and Model* (Florida State University Tallahassee Center for Educational Technology, 1975), www.dtic.mil/dtic/tr/fulltext/u2/a019486.pdf.

19. SWOT ANALYSIS: Your Library's Strengths, Weaknesses, Opportunities, and Threats, www.ala.org/advocacy/swot-analysis-your-librarys-strengths-weaknesses-opportunities -and-threats.

CHAPTER 8

....

SUSTAINING
SERVICE AS A VALUE

....

Good leadership, whether formal or informal, is helping other people rise to
their full potential while accomplishing the mission and goals of the organization. All members of an organization, who are responsible for the work of
others, have the potential to be good leaders if properly developed.
—*Bob Mason*[1]

The service leadership values discussed in previous chapters have focused
on individual efforts to model service. This chapter will focus on how
to sustain the service organization culture. In order for an organization,
such as a library, to sustain a service culture, it must embed the vision and values
in all of its efforts; they must become part of its organizational identity, part of
policies, procedures, and the internal governance systems such as evaluation and
project management.

The service culture is built on the vision and purpose of the organization. All
other values and activities are dependent on this commitment of service being
a shared vision. For the organization to sustain this vision, individuals must be
committed to it as well. Service leaders help advocate for this vision and get other
individuals involved and move them toward a desired future.

DEFINING THE PURPOSE AND VISION

Perhaps the single most effective unifying factor in an organization is its purpose.
A purpose is the reason the library exists, its reason for being, that unites all the
individuals in an organization. Northouse asserts that it is the leader who "influences a group of individuals to achieve a common goal."[2] After all, people will
choose to work for an organization and a leader that aligns with their own values.
This is particularly true in a public service organization, where the focus is on
the public good and the values of the organization reflect that purpose. In public
service organizations, service is obviously the defining value. However, it is curious that such an organization may limit its service ethic to the public and treat its

employees as something less, as collegiality that is not a service in itself. This says something about the organization that is not very positive.

Vision is the potential of an organization that reflects its purpose and values. It is the building of community values that is key: call it climate or organizational culture, but it is the internalization of these service leadership values that sustain them. It is the role of leadership to frame the values for the organization and to socialize employees into them: "A common goal requires that the leader and followers agree on the direction to be taken by the group."[3]

There are a number of efforts, functions, and practices used to sustain an established service-oriented organization, but the key to sustaining it is the organization's culture and, specifically, its defining culture of purpose—a commitment to service both within and outside the organization. This culture empowers the organization to "strategize its promises, design its processes, and engage its people in a proactive quest for competitive advantage."[4] Lueneburger supports this by asserting that "cultures of purpose power winning organizations. And although leaders are right to track innovation, differentiation, and profitability, it is in the cultures of purpose that any of these last."[5]

The culture of purpose is critical, but how is it determined and sustained? In many cases the purpose is intertwined with the mission and vision statement of the library. This is only true, however, if the mission statement is more than a political document. So often the mission and vision statements may be reflective of the director rather than an expression of what the organization is truly committed to. If those with management authority in the library make top-down decisions about service standards and values, then they ignore the library team and individuals on the front line whose jobs are to serve patrons and the public in light of those standards. Will this new mission and vision be embraced and sustained by the team? Probably not, particularly if they don't value it. Consequently, how will this director, who has positional authority, sustain the new library's culture? Particularly, when employees "see something going right or wrong with a group or organization and then attribute the result to the leader."[6] If employees do not believe in their director's vision and mission, how can the organization's new culture and the purpose of the organization be sustained?

ADVOCATING SERVICE LEADERSHIP

There are many studies in the management and psychology literature that report that the top leadership sets the tone. Although, leadership certainly has a huge impact on the organizational climate, it is the employees that sustain the culture. This means that even a mid-level manager can have a huge effect, positive or negative, on sustaining the service culture. How important is it, personally, to have a manager that you can trust and respect and who is supportive? The literature says that the number-one reason that people leave their job is their supervisor—even if everything else in the work environment is okay. Regardless of how much a person professionally accomplishes, how fulfilled she may feel by successfully performing her job duties, and how committed to the organization she is, it is impossible to entirely compartmentalize the negativity of a bad leadership relationship.

It may be that the direct supervisor is very supportive, respected, and trusted—and may be an effective buffer between the individual employee and the administration. However, a supervisor cannot filter everything—and as they may try to protect their direct employees, it has the potential to make it worse. Because such an action could engender loyalty to the manager but a sense of unfairness with the administration, particularly as an employee sees how it could negatively impact their manager.

What you do has more impact than what you say—ideally, they should be consistent. In the absence of that, it is a truism but no less true that actions will speak louder than words.

The classic leader in libraries has been influenced by the traditional hierarchical structure, which has been largely unchanged in the profession, even if everything else is in flux. The communication style may be directive; the supervisory style authoritarian, and the organization rule-bound, with the leader focused on command and control. Leaders, particularly those with a vision-of-service orientation, will strive to create an organization that fits that image. When authority is concentrated in the top of an organization, the vision and direction change with the leadership, which may ultimately impact climate and engagement. A leader who is more focused on status or power will try to remake the organization in his own image, build a power base, and do whatever it takes to make himself look good. A service leader will make an effort to align their behavior with the foundational values of the organization and lead through shared governance, promoting buy-in and sustainability. So, how can service leadership be sustained in an organization regardless of the authority at the top?

We have previously discussed other values, characteristics, and behavior that are indicative of service leadership and help to create a service climate. Greenleaf highlighted some of these values when he stated, "There really is a set of values, a sense of *fairness, honesty, respect,* and *contribution* that transcends culture—something that is timeless that transcends the ages and that is also self-evident. It is as self-evident as the requirement of trustworthiness to produce trust."[7] His reference to trust is a significant one, because it is fundamental to the integrity of a service leader and it also is critical to sustaining a service culture.

BUILDING AN ENVIRONMENT OF TRUST

Building an environment of trust—this sounds like it is pretty easy, right? After all, everyone is committed to service and has good intentions. However, this may be the single most difficult area to address. And if an organization has trust issues, it is difficult, but not impossible, for employees to recover. There are a number of issues that influence trust, including equity and favoritism, transparency in decision-making and procedural justice.

Those in positional authority have a certain right by virtue of that authority, and they have a job to do just like everyone else. However, sometimes the exercise of this authority is done in such a way that employees feel victimized. Just as surprising your boss is to be avoided, management by ambush is an equally bad idea. Colin Powell raises this concern in the context of what is a standard practice in organizations: "I avoid reorganizations like the plague. They are something that you do *to* somebody rather than *for* somebody."[8]

In organizations, individuals who voice concern may be considered detractors, rabble-rousers, or change resistant. Interestingly, this says less about the individuals who question managerial decisions and more about the decision-makers and the culture of the organization. Instead of marginalizing individuals who have questions, concerns or differing opinions, they could be brought into the process early, which could result in a better outcome: "Often potential problems or resistance can be reduced or even eliminated by including in the decision-making process itself those most likely to be affected."[9] Haass describes the concept of inoculating those who may be impacted by change, letting them participate in the planning of it so they are prepared.[10] This not only makes the change more likely to succeed, but it also gains the trust of the team and ultimately sustains the service culture.

There have been numerous references to teams in libraries, and teaming has been a trend in the business literature, although that is not why it is so prevalent in libraries. Librarianship, by its very nature, is a very collaborative endeavor. As a basic example, look at the number of library staff that process a book, from those who make the request and place the order to those who receive and catalog it. Many of the services in libraries are very interdependent, with each individual playing a different role and making a different contribution to the whole effort. The team can act as a microcosm for the larger organization or it can be a cohesive unit. Part of the benefit of teams is the diversity that it brings to organizational efforts. In most cases, diversity is viewed as a social construct, those "explicit differences among group members in social category membership, such as race, gender and ethnicity."[11] While this definition of diversity is the most recognized and, for organizations, the most concerning because of organizational values or the potential legal situations around protected classes. Perhaps it is natural that there are different types of diversity as well. Informational diversity "refers to differences in knowledge bases and perspectives that members bring to the group."[12] Value diversity "occurs when members of a workgroup differ in terms of what they think the group's real task, goal, target, or mission should be."[13] In other words, groups may have differing opinions and expectations that can impact their effectiveness. That said, it is widely accepted that while diversity can create conflict, it can also bring issues to the surface that result in a more successful outcome. Different perspectives bring up different issues and implications, potentially identifying weaknesses or gaps in a plan.

Another issue around building an environment of trust is transparency, which is a buzzword right along with big government. Transparency is one way to assure that everyone is aware of the process, that there is nothing questionable about what you are about to do. This can be done before you implement change by asking yourself not only: "whether what you are doing or are planning to do passes a legal test, but also whether it passes the smell test . . . If it does not feel right, if it could cause serious problems, forget it."[14] If you can't defend an action or a decision with sincerity, then don't do it because it will affect your trust relationship with your employees.

Respect is another value that is highly embedded in the concept of service and is critical to sustaining the service organizational culture. An organization that values respect and cares for its patrons should also model this value for its employees. Too often there is a disconnect between how patrons and employees are treated, and this undermines the true value of the organization. The service ethic of respect should be modeled in all situations because the "leader appreciates the professional, personal, and spiritual dimensions of each person's life outside of the tangible everyday efforts of the individual in the workplace."[15] While this may sound too warm and fuzzy, there are many studies that indicate that employees who feel respected and empowered provide better patron service and are more engaged in the organization, ultimately benefiting that organization and sustaining the created culture. Senge supported the idea of respect when he quoted the president of an insurance company, "Our traditional organizations are designed to provide for the first three levels of Maslow's hierarchy of human needs: food, shelter, and belonging. Since these are now widely available to members of industrial society, our organizations do not provide significantly unique opportunities to command the loyalty and commitment of our people. The ferment in management will continue until organizations begin to address the higher order needs: self-respect and self-actualization."[16] Having an organization with leaders who believe that it is their job to help employees succeed has a lot of impact. Jeremy Brandt, CEO of FastHomeOffers.com, began asking questions. What problems do you have? How can I help you? . . . "At the company, I solve people's problems," he says. "I give them what they need so they can grow and blossom."[17]

Respect for employees can be shown in the way that credit is given. In organizations in which authority is closely held at the top, very little decision-making is delegated to the employees, regardless of how much they know. Consequently, those in positional authority tend to claim the credit for successes (and conversely, push the blame down) when they had little or no involvement in them. This kind of environment is diametrically opposed to a service culture. When titled leadership signals that this kind of culture is the norm, it can have implications for other behaviors such as harassment and bullying.

> Although the focus is on the individual, the larger picture—the library's mission—remains important. Its importance is tempered, however, by the view that when the vital pieces receive priority, the others will fall into place . . . If the [servant leader] (1) focuses on the needs of employees; (2) expects, encourages, and models results through valuing relationships; and (3) recognizes people for their contributions, the likely outcome will be a greater sense of trust and accountability, leading to more risk-taking, creativity, and innovation. This in turn will create a strong team that multiplies its abilities to meet customer needs; it will also increase empowerment of individuals to solve problems at the grassroots level. The solutions will be better, there will be increased feelings of self-worth, and productivity will be higher."[18]

As indicated, organizational hierarchy has profound implications for setting a service culture. A flatter organization that distributes responsibility and encourages empowerment will be more effective in providing service as well.

PERFORMANCE

Once the service culture has been implemented, the service leader must ensure that all her employees and users clearly understand what the service culture is, how it will be provided, and the standards in which it is to be delivered as a way of sustaining the culture. In order to achieve this consistent service delivery, the service leader will need to establish measures that are understood, shared, performed, and achieved by both employees and patrons.

In the following vignette, one can see that the service culture broke down because the employee did not follow a consistent service delivery protocol that was clearly understood by the second library patron. Exceptional service is a goal, but by definition, it is an exception. This inconsistency in protocol, while it ben-

SERVICE LEADERSHIP IN PRACTICE

At noon Paul walks up to the reserves desk and asks to check out a book that is on reserve for his 211 engineering class. Paul, a slow reader, quickly realizes that the loan period for the item is only two hours, and he will not be able to complete the reading before the textbook is due. Paul looks up to the librarian and asks if she can make an exception because he needs the item longer. The librarian looks at Paul and, without checking to see if there was a waiting list for the piece, allowed Paul an extra two hours. At two o'clock Desmond walks up to the reserve desk and asks for the same 211 engineering textbook so that he can do the assigned reading. The librarian says that someone already had taken the item out at noon and that it would be back at four o'clock that afternoon. Shocked, Desmond says, "I thought that it was a two-hour checkout, and when I asked to check the textbook out yesterday for more than two hours you told me 'no.' My name was on the waiting list to get the item at two this afternoon. This is unfair." Desmond turns away from the desk and goes to the library's administration office to complain about the breach in delivery of service.

efits one patron, may then bring up questions of equity or procedural justice for others. The waiting list was a method to provide a more service-oriented effort, but it was circumvented. The failure in service culture was noted when the second library patron went to the administration office to give the library director feedback on the botched service interaction.

DEVELOPMENT AND MENTORING

The investment of time and money in programs such as training and mentoring can be considerable, but the payoff may be less tangible and identifiable. However, this is a perspective that it both short-sighted and focused on the profit-motive. "Training is not an expense but an investment."[19]

Far too often organizational leaders struggle to understand the importance of mentoring in the effort to create a learning organization. They brush off the idea that employees need to develop their professional knowledge and encourage them to do it on their own time, not company time. They fail to recognize that, as times change, so do their employees' skill levels. In order to stay competitive and relevant, their employees' skills must match or exceed those needed to meet the changing environment. What this means is that employees must continually update their knowledge. When leaders turn their back on professional development, some employees take it as a sign that the leaders of the organization do not care about their future and, consequently, the employees may become unwilling to expend the additional time or money to update their core skills for an uncaring company. How does this affect the company? When they are hired, employees are highly skilled for the position that they hold, but as time passes and things change, their skill level and knowledge remains where it was when they were first hired. Without updating their core skills through professional development, the job opportunities for these employees within the company become restricted because the discrepancy between what they can and cannot do increases. The gap in job tasks requires the organization to continue to pay wages for unqualified people to do the jobs that may no longer be needed and to hire in new talent, at a higher wage that has the necessary skills and expertise.

It is important to look at organizational learning in order to cultivate the service-oriented outlook within the organization, to improve the employees' knowledge which is required to provide exceptional patron service and as a way to continual developmental training and coaching in order to sustain the patron service organizational culture. Openness to learning is critical in a service-driven organization because change is necessary to be responsive to those you serve. Continuous change requires not just effective but outstanding leadership. This is not limited to the individual at the top of the organization or to those in management positions but includes anyone who has an opportunity to contribute to the organization, serve the public, and collaborate as part of a team. Improving a specific aspect of development, such a communication skills, can ultimately lead to proficiency in other aspects of service leadership and, in turn, prompt others within the organization to improve as well: " . . . enhancement of a leader's communication attitudes and practices might facilitate servant leader formation."[20]

This service leadership model is the antithesis of traditional academic libraries, which are procedurally based and hierarchically organized and reduces organization commitment.[21] Research indicates that team-based structures are preferable to a hierarchy; a flatter organizational structure that embraces shared governance would be more effective.

It is critical to establish integrity in the change process, at both an organizational and an individual level, and build support for organizational goals. In order to achieve these goals, a service leader is critical of his own beliefs while making the effort to know and understand his employees' beliefs and concerns related to the mission of the library. This knowledge gives a service leader the information needed to anticipate changing environments and communicate these changes before or as they are happening so that employees can continually improve.[22] Change is never easy, however, and the service leader needs to focus on what the will of the group is by being attentive to his surroundings. As a result, the service leader can anticipate the needs of the employee before the he or she lets the service leader know.

The service leader provides an environment in which there is trust, nurturance, and empathy, an environment in which the employee is coached rather than punished for the risks she took to solve difficult issues, even if her efforts failed. "In a supportive context, followers feel safe to confront hard problems."[23]

Senge's concept of a learning organization is descriptive of a transformational organization, "What fundamentally will distinguish learning organizations from traditional authoritarian 'controlling organizations' will be the mastery of certain principles."[24] Among these principles are personal mastery (competency), mental models and shared vision, team learning, and systems thinking. This paradigm also aligns well with service organizations in its responsiveness. Finally, because it requires continuous learning and assessment, it also has affinity with the purpose of higher education and academic libraries. The fundamental focus is responsiveness and growth.

A very traditional model of instructional design is not unrelated to the ADDIE model mentioned in chapter 7. This model comes from a military background and looks at analysis, design, development, implementation, and evaluation. Note that it begins with analysis and ends with evaluation, both of which are focused on assessment of the situation or project. In this way it closes the loop on the continuous learning process. The time for reflection and intention is critical. This model is usually centered around a project, and assessment is often tied to a formal effort or metric. But assessment can also be a process of slowing down, stop and smell the roses, breathe and contemplate. It is also an opportunity to check in with peers or employees, to renew the connection and see how they are This can lead to realizations that may be more profound than a measurement.

There are times when mentoring and developing individuals may be indicated by "helping them out of the organization." This may happen for any number of reasons, but the major drivers are related to person-organization fit or performance. First, if an individual has different values or expectations than the organization, it is probably in everyone's best interest to have a conversation about the mismatch; it may be that a compromise can be reached. If not, however, that individual may be more successful in another organization. The second possibility is related to performance and opportunity. The obvious take on that is that the individual is not performing (thus has no opportunity) and should be shown the door. The less obvious circumstance, but one that happens more often than people may recognize, is when a high performer who continues to excel and grow tops out. The response to this situation is one that is highly emblematic of a service leadership value: the high performing, committed individual should be encouraged in her growth even if it takes her to a different organization.

ASSESSMENT AND FEEDBACK

Encouragement and accountability are both necessary elements and were discussed previously in theory. Perhaps the most critical system related to performance assessment and feedback is the reward system (or, conversely, those processes related to sanctioning or remediation). People tend to do what they are rewarded for. If a librarian sees that people gets raises (or promotions) for behaving in a certain way or performing a certain task, he is likely to do it as well, regardless of whether the desirable behavior has been articulated in the strategic plan or even individual goals. By the same token, if a librarian puts in a lot of time on an exhibition or program but it is largely overlooked by those who evaluate and give rewards, he is unlikely to put himself out again. Skinner's reinforcement theory and extinction theory both indicate that feedback is key to either maintaining or changing behavior.

Leban and Stone state that there are nine key employee motivators that can be used in an empowered environment:

- material rewards—seeking possessions, wealth, and a high standard of living;
- power/influence—seeking to be in control of people and resources;
- search for meaning—seeking to do things that are believed valuable for their own sake;
- expertise—seeking a high level of accomplishment in a specialized field;
- creativity—seeking to innovate and be identified with original output;
- affiliation—seeking nourishing relationship with others;
- autonomy—seeking to be independent and able to make decisions for oneself;
- security—seeking a solid and predictable future;
- status—seeking to be recognized, admired, and respected from the community at large.[25]

The first couple of motivators or rewards listed above are the ones that are regularly employed in organizations and tend to be the most obvious. They can be correlated with merit, raises, and promotions, those tangible indicators of success in the organization. However, they are not motivators in and of themselves. In fact, as Frederick Herzberg's theory indicates, they are demotivators.[26] Tangible rewards such as raises are considered hygiene factors and are ephemeral: the glow from a raise lasts as long as the individual considers it new—which is only about as long as it takes him to get used to it. Motivators, particularly for those individuals drawn to a service organization, are likely to be more in the realm of higher order needs, as defined by Maslow.[27]

SYSTEMATIZING INNOVATION AND CHANGE

Innovation may also be a value in an organization. Certainly, with the advances in technology, many organizations, libraries among them, explore the possibilities of how to employ technology. The interesting thing is, so often, technology is the driver for innovations in service; however the effort should be driven by what the customer needs and technology may be the vehicle or the means for meeting that need. Otherwise, innovation is being developed in a vacuum—and it is not a case of "If you build it, they will come."

In order to successfully transform an organization, the traditional model of top-down decision-making and behavior must be unlearned in order for services to be constantly questioned and enhanced, aligning them with the service culture:

> . . . the largest gap between the principles of quality and the library may come in the aspect of employee involvement in decision-making. Libraries have relied on comprehensive policies and standardized procedures to eliminate the need for individual decisions. The value of consistency has sometimes outweighed the value of customer satisfaction. The emphasis has been on quality control instead of quality improvement.[28]

A more inclusive approach to organizational management can more effectively manage change. "Distributed power, open and decentralized communication systems, participative decision-making, and acceptance of conflict have been identified as contributing to successful changes."[29] This shift to a more collaborative effort builds community and shared interest. Kovel-Jarboe goes on to discuss barriers or resistance to change:

1. "Perception that the change would interfere with future promotions.
2. Reasons for change were not clear to those expected to change most.
3. Perception that the change was not important to continued success.
4. Change decreased or eliminated rewarding aspects of jobs.
5. Change not compatible with prevailing values.
6. People felt coerced to adopt change.
7. A hostile working climate existed in the organization.

8. Resistance to change was not dealt with constructively.
9. Functional or territorial boundaries prevented collaboration.
10. Sponsors of the planned change lacked agreement on key goals."[30]

These efforts are not just transformational in the organization but for individuals as well: "In moving toward mutual goals, both the leader and the followers are changed."[31] While it may seem like a chicken-or-egg question, it is truly about openness to change and to learning.

BUILDING COMMUNITY, STEWARDSHIP AND SUSTAINING

Organizational citizenship, which Vondey defines as interpersonal helping, individual initiative, personal industry, and loyal boosterism, is consistent with service and stewardship.[32] This is distinct from regular expectations because "individuals have discretion in the degree to which they comply."[33] Kathleen Patterson put it eloquently with her statement that servant leaders "seek to serve the future."[34]

But a critical factor in this attribute is how to sustain it within the organization. Sustainability is now a loaded term that conjures images of old growth forests and the ongoing debate between tree-huggers and consumers. Lueneburger discusses the sustainability of organizations, and while he is referring to sustainability in the environmental sense, he is also referring to sustainability in terms of the survival and success of the organization itself. But sustainability is also a service-oriented effort with a focus on purpose: "Because it captures an ideal, a purpose goes beyond profitable growth, shareholder value, or any other measure of whether you are doing things right. A purpose, instead, is a pledge to *do the right things.*"[35]

It also has a definition related particularly to service organizations and their fundamental purpose, that stewardship or to "hold something in trust for another" is a responsibility for the individuals and the organization. This is significant to the purpose and its perpetuation:

"Senge contended that one of the important tasks of leaders in learning organizations is to be the steward (servant) of the vision within the organization. Being a steward means clarifying and nurturing a vision that is greater than oneself. This means not being self-centered, but rather integrating one's self or vision with that of others in the organization. Effective leaders see their own personal vision as part of something larger than themselves—a part of the organization and the community at large."[36]

SERVICE LEADERSHIP IN PRACTICE

Logan, a new web designer, was hired to develop a state-of-the-art web-site for a large academic library. During his interview it was stressed that the organizational environment and culture was one of encouragement and creative thinking, where a person was supported and not penalized when employees took risks even when the risk didn't pay off. However, two weeks after Logan was hired, he began to perceive behavior—specifically, his boss' attitude toward risk-taking—that was completely opposite of what he'd been told. Logan began seeing his boss penalizing other team members for taking risks and even chastising employees openly during meetings for taking risks, saying that "they should not have taken such a careless risk." Gradually, Logan began to believe that the tolerant environment he thought he was working in didn't actually exist. He realized the organizational culture that the leader continually espoused was not real and that creative thinking, whether the person was successful or not, was actually frowned on instead of celebrated.

Dupree offers a detailed list of signs that an organization is in entropy (stagnation), including a tendency toward superficiality; tension among key people; lack of time for celebration; differing definitions of *service, trust,* or *responsibility;* more problem-makers than problem-solvers; a focus on control rather than liberation; loss of grace and civility; reliance on structures rather than people; considering customers as impositions rather than opportunities to serve.[37]

Lueneburger discusses sustainability, focusing on handprints as opposed to footprints. "Instead of focusing on reducing bad unintended consequences, let's talk about maximizing the positive impact we can actively pursue as a primary objective. Convey your information in the context of what can be done *beneficially* rather than in the negative context of what has to stop."[38] He also addresses some signs of success in terms of sustaining purpose, stating that the "goals are so clear and they've been embraced so completely that people take it upon themselves to do something."[39] Changes may occur, small or large, that align with the purpose but without the managers knowing; "when the culture of purpose is so ingrained in the company that it starts to spread the message outward to customers and vendors."[40]

Libraries and other service organizations, because of their role as a public good, have this responsibility as well. Sustainability may be indicated in the performance of employees and their adherence to service leadership values: "The signs of outstanding leadership appear primarily among the followers. Are the followers reaching their potential? Are they learning? Serving? Do they achieve the required results? Do they change with grace? Manage conflict?"[41] More broadly, these criteria show sustainability:

- evangelizing the culture—how patrons can perpetuate it;
- commitment to the future of the organization; and
- building of the library community.

Sustaining can also refer to following through—that is, doing what you say at an individual level and, at an organizational level, fulfilling your purpose. Developing and sustaining these principles takes intention and commitment. Leadership models are like diet programs; they come and go, advocating various philosophies or practices that an individual or an organization may observe for a while. But either reality intrudes and they revert to their traditional behavior or they assume the next flavor-of-the-month fad. Just as self-help and diet programs have started to underscore the need for a lifestyle change, leadership ideologies, to be successful, must create an environment that fosters the principles they espouse but one that can sustain them.

REFLECTIONS ON SUSTAINING: TOOLS FOR DEVELOPMENT

1. Think about your biggest successes, where you have had the most positive impact. As you think of them, are they projects or are they people?
2. As you think about other individuals you have worked with, how many other leaders have you grown or nurtured?
3. Change places with someone in your group for a day.
4. In considering your vision, surface your assumptions. What are the implications of these?
5. Thinks about how you treat your patrons. What is the service standard in the organization?
6. With that service standard in mind, do you treat your colleagues within the organization the same way? Is there a different standard of service internally?

NOTES

1. Dan McCarthy, "What Is Leadership? 30 Definitions," http://management.about.com/od/leadership/fl/What-is-Leadership-30-Definitions.htm.
2. Peter G. Northouse, *Leadership: Theory and Practice,* 6th ed. (Thousand Oaks, CA: Sage Publications, 2013), 15.
3. Ibid., 436.
4. Svafa Grönfeldt and Judith Strother, *Service Leadership: The Quest for Competitive Advantage* (Thousand Oaks, CA: Sage Publications, 2006), 79.
5. Christoph Lueneburger, *A Culture of Purpose: How to Choose the Right People and Make the Right People Choose You* (San Francisco, CA: Jossey-Bass, 2014), 1.
6. Joseph S. Nye, Jr., *Powers to Lead* (New York, NY: Oxford University Press, 2008), 3.
7. Robert K. Greenleaf, *Servant Leadership: A Journey into the Nature of Legitimate Power & Greatness* (Mahwah, NJ: Paulist, 1977), 5.
8. Richard N. Haass, *The Bureaucratic Entrepreneur: How to Be Effective in Any Unruly Organization* (Washington, DC: Brookings Institution, 1999), 92.
9. Ibid., 42.
10. Ibid.
11. Karen A. Jehn, Gregory B. Northcraft, and Margaret A. Neale, "Why Differences Make a Difference: A Field Study of Diversity, Conflict and Performance in Workgroups," *Administrative Science Quarterly* 44, no. 4 (1999): 745.
12. Ibid., 743.
13. Ibid., 745.
14. Richard N. Haass, *The Bureaucratic Entrepreneur: How to be Effective in Any Unruly Organization* (Washington, DC: Brookings Institution, 1999), 51.
15. Filippa Marullo Anzalone, "Servant Leadership: A New Model for Law Library Leaders," *Law Library Journal* 99 no. 4 (2007): 802.
16. Peter M. Senge, *The Fifth Discipline: The Art & Practice of the Learning Organization* (New York, NY: Doubleday, 1990), 347.
17. Leigh Buchanan, "In Praise of Selflessness: Why the Best Leaders are Servants," *Inc Magazine* (May 2007): 35.
18. John Doncevic, "Servant-Leadership as a Model for Library Administration," *Catholic Library World* 73, no. 3 (2003): 173.
19. Al Gore, "World Class Courtesy: A Best Practices Report," *A Report of the National Performance Review* National Performance Review (US), and Albert Gore, *World-class Courtesy: A Best Practices Report: A Report of the National Performance Review.* (The Review, 1997), 8.
20. Mark A. Rennaker, *Listening and Persuasion: Examining the Communicative Patterns of Servant Leadership* (Regent University, 2008), 2.
21. Song Yang, "A Contextual Analysis of Organizational Commitment," *Sociological Focus* 36, no. 1 (2003): 49–64.
22. Fons Trompenaars and Ed Voerman, *Servant-Leadership Across Cultures* (New York, NY: McGraw Hill, 2010), 37–38.
23. Peter G. Northouse, *Leadership: Theory and Practice,* 6th ed. (Thousand Oaks, CA: Sage Publications, 2013), 429.

24. Peter M. Senge, *The Fifth Discipline: The Art & Practice of the Learning Organization* (New York, NY: Doubleday, 1990), 5.

25. Bill Leban and Romuald Stone, *Managing Organizational Change,* 2nd ed. (Hoboken, NJ: John Wiley, 2008), 136.

26. Fredrick I Herzberg, *Work and the Nature of Man* (Cleveland, OH: World Publishing, 1966).

27. Abraham Harold Maslow, "A Theory of Human Motivation," *Psychological Review* 50, no. 4 (1943): 370.

28. Patricia Kovel-Jarboe, "Quality Improvement: A Strategy for Planned Organizational Change," *Library Trends* 44, no. 3 (1996): 610.

29. Ibid., 612.

30. Ibid., 613.

31. Peter G. Northouse, *Leadership: Theory and Practice,* 6th ed. (Thousand Oaks, CA: Sage Publications, 2013), 437

32. Michelle Vondey, "The Relationships Among Servant Leadership, Organizational Citizenship Behavior, Person-Organization Fit, and Organizational Identification," *International Journal of Leadership Studies* 6, no. 1 (2010): 3.

33. Ibid., 5.

34. Kathleen A. Patterson, "Servant Leadership: A Theoretical Model," (dissertation, Regent University, 2003), 7.

35. Christoph Lueneburger, *A Culture of Purpose: How to Choose the Right People and Make the Right People Choose You* (San Francisco, CA: Jossey-Bass, 2014), 2

36. Peter G. Northouse, *Introduction to Leadership: Concepts and Practice* (Thousand Oaks, CA: Sage Publications, 2009), 388.

37. Max Dupree, *Leadership Is an Art* (East Lansing, Mich.: Michigan State University Press, 1987), 111–112.

38. Christoph Lueneburger, *A Culture of Purpose: How to Choose the Right People and Make the Right People Choose You* (San Francisco, CA: Jossey-Bass, 2014), 25.

39. Ibid., 23

40. Ibid., 24

41. Max Dupree *Leadership is an Art* (East Lansing, Mich.: Michigan State University Press, 1987), 12.

CHAPTER 9

FORMALIZING SERVICE LEADERSHIP IN LIBRARIES

Embedding Processes and Policies

Employees who believe that management is concerned about
them as a whole person—not just an employee—are more
productive, more satisfied, more fulfilled. Satisfied employees
mean satisfied customers, which leads to profitability.
—*Anne M. Mulcahy, former CEO of Xerox*[1]

In order to sustain a service leadership organization, the internal policies and
practices must reflect that commitment. Undeniably, it is those with management authority who determine the policies and procedures in an organization; hence they tend to have the best chance of success in instituting a service
culture (or other paradigmatic changes). These are clear indicators of the cultural
values and climate in the organization; they may, or may not, be aligned with
the explicit mission statements and values documents. The ideal, of course, is
that they would be. The values or mission may espouse service values while the
policies are more focused on following the rules. When there is this disconnect,
the impact on the organization can be profound; individuals may be confused,
unsure about what the priorities are, and frustrated. Sometimes the lack of success is due to not following through. But sometimes it is because the values of
the organization and the desired change are not aligned—they are not a good
fit. Does this mean that an organization that is very hierarchical and authoritarian with a tendency toward micromanagement and risk-averse behavior cannot
change? Of course not. But it does mean that the organizational values and the
organizational behavior need to be explicitly examined and discussed, and all
parts of the organization need to be included.

The overall transformation of leadership in an organization can be increased
substantially by suitable organizational and human resources policies.[2] "Transformational leadership presents opportunities for improving the organization's
image, recruitment, selection, promotion, management of diversity, teamwork,

training, development, and ability to innovate."[3] It also frames the context for a sustained environment. Covey asks, "How do you get this concern for the individual customer? I see three ways: hire it, train it, or cultivate it in the culture."[4] Having the values of the organization permeate every policy, every process, demonstrates that the organization is committed. There are opportunities everywhere, and nowhere are they more obvious than in human resources:

- hiring and promotion;
- training and development;
- career development and succession planning;
- job design and workload;
- performance evaluation; and
- rewards and compensation.

These policies, among others, inform employees' relationships with and perceptions of the organization. How it handles more conflict-laden situations, such as termination, disciplinary action, or grievances, says something about how the organization comports itself. Just as an individual's response to negative circumstances says the most about him, so does an organization's response to its problems. If it models integrity and service, that exemplifies its values.

Human resources (HR) may have a bad reputation internally in an organization among those it is there to serve. At worst employees can view HR's role as covering for the organization, pushing paper, and forcing time-consuming and unnecessary procedures down everyone's throat. There are HR offices that believe this is their role and responsibility and that they are there to manage those human resources (which seems somewhat dehumanizing when people are managed as assets or inventory). However, service leaders recognize that this view can be altered for the positive and that employees do not have to feel this way, especially if HR efforts focus on the service ethic of the library.

> I spent more than 25 years as a corporate head of HR in large corporations and currently consult in the field. Last year I attended a conference where the Container Store shared how it trains and develops employees. There is no HR department, but there is an HR function that originally was part of the marketing department. This caught my attention as I have been arguing for some time that effective HR needs to be a marketing effort. Marketing builds brands. Many companies spend little time helping develop and market their people. The real value of human-resource management is identifying, recruiting, managing, developing, retaining and compensating people to help build successful businesses and brands.[5]

In this chapter, we will examine the processes that can model organizational values from the beginning of the employee-employer relationship through the various relationship ends, and what their implications are for the formalization of values for the organization as a whole.

RECRUITMENT AND SELECTION

It can readily be argued that people who value service are drawn to service organizations. While hiring is not necessarily the most important action to impact an organization, its culture, and its success, it is arguably the most visible. Every organization wants to hire the best and brightest. The hiring process is not just about weeding through applicants to get the best, however; it is also necessary for the organization to make a good impression. How the process is conducted says a lot about the organization to the candidates.

It starts with the framing of the position description, which indicates the job design and workload. Candidates have significant questions and the position description or position announcement helps them answer these (or not, which can be an answer in itself):

1. How much autonomy does it have?
2. Who does It collaborate with?
3. What are the priorities?
4. How does this position fit into the organization?

These are all questions that the organization has answered within the position description, which is the first attractor for potential hires. If the position description is very narrowly written, it is an indicator that there is an internal candidate; this will deter many experienced librarians and high performers from applying. The question about how the position fits into the organization raises the more significant question about fit; while most organizations are looking at candidates to see how well they fit the position, most candidates are looking at the organization to determine how well they might fit within its culture. Overlooking the fact that potential hires are interviewing the organization is a colossal, yet common, mistake that many hiring organizations make. There are organizations that pay attention to this detail as well: they coach their employees to be positive and sell the organization, as if the library were being interviewed by the candidate (and let's be honest, it is). Unfortunately, this strategy has some significant pitfalls as well, particularly if the candidate is chosen and takes the position. After the honeymoon period, however long that may be, the recruited individual will discover the real culture in the organization and likely feel that she was fooled. Hosting candidates professionally is advised, but it is also in everyone's best interest to have a realistic job (and organization) preview. If the organization has issues that it does not feel would attract a candidate, this is probably an excellent indication that this issue needs to be addressed and remediated within the organization.

SERVICE LEADERSHIP IN PRACTICE

Jason was hired into the college library as a law librarian. He had initially applied for a senior librarian position, but the college library had three very strong applicants so they hired all three at entry level. While this was unusual and not what he anticipated, Jason was excited to get the job at a place that would invest so heavily in his subject area. After a couple of years, one of his colleagues left. The position went unfilled and unposted until the director of the library decided to invite a librarian who she was mentoring to interview for senior librarian. Jason and his colleague were both upset at this turn of events; it was the position that they both had initially interviewed for but instead had been offered the entry-level position. Both were interested in applying for the senior library position and, without a posting, they would not get the chance.

The candidate, Pamela, interviewed with the director and other librarians. Comments were minimal and noncontroversial, except for Jason and his colleague, who asked probing questions about the candidate's experience and vision. The candidate was indignant about what she called their aggressive demeanor and told the director about it. The director scheduled a meeting with Jason and his colleague, during which she chastised them. She said that their behavior was not appropriate, that this was not the way to treat candidates, and that they were entirely unsuited for the job anyway. She then asserted that the director can hire whomever she wants and it didn't matter what they thought.

Pamela was hired as senior librarian, supervising Jason and his colleague. Jason's colleague quit two days later. Jason followed after a couple of months, sending a scathing letter to the college president. While this situation may have been specific to the organization, the fact that these individuals left because of it indicates that it is likely to be news in the larger professional community as well.

Speaking of internal candidates, the hiring process also sends signals to employees in the organization. If, as in the above example, a position is written with one specific employee in mind, this can, and will, send a message to other employees about the objectivity and fairness of the process. It can lead to accusations of favoritism (or more likely dissatisfied grumbling), and in extreme cases, it can completely undermine trust in the hiring process and in the decision-makers.

There are number of issues in this case: the initial interviews and decision to hire three candidates into lower-level positions than what they applied for, the decision not to post the senior librarian position, bringing in someone with whom the director had an existing relationship to interview for an unposted position, and taking input from affected individuals but being very resistant to any feedback. In addition, Pamela exacerbated the situation and perpetuated the issues of procedural justice while subverting the process by going to her mentor, the director. While she ultimately gets the position, her credibility is undermined and she is not trusted by anyone in the organization who witnessed this. Another issue that is most relevant to hiring but may be overlooked because of the blatant favoritism is the dilemma around Jason's hire, that the position he applied for was not the one that he ultimately was offered and that it was a lower-level job. This bait-and-switch tactic makes an impression on Jason, his colleagues, and others in the organization. While administrators may say that each situation is unique, it sends a message about fairness and the values.

As alluded to in the situation above, the interaction in the interview accounts for a lot. It is largely accepted that 70 percent (or more) of communication is nonverbal, and so being able to watch the candidate's reactions, mannerisms, and demeanor is very revealing. The reverse is also true, that being, how employees and managers within the organization interact with candidates. Those brief interactions say a lot about the organization at large and influence a candidate's decision to accept a job offer or not. Legally, there are questions that you can and cannot ask, but beyond that, the questions asked and conversations pursued in an interview are telling about what is important to the organization, how it approaches situations, how engaged its employees are, and how valued they feel. Many organizations do training about hiring to avoid legal entanglements, but many also coach their employees to put on a good face. This is a little ironic—if you have satisfied and motivated employees, they don't need that kind of coaching. In addition, in terms of the integrity of the process, it is a little shift—kind of like selling a used car.

LEARNING AND PERSONNEL DEVELOPMENT

We will make an assumption about sustaining a service culture—that these practices can be taught or inculcated into new hires. Bass argued that transformational leadership behaviors can be learned, and Haass said "technique can be taught," although *taught* is probably too concrete a word.[6] It is really a process of socialization. It begins with the job posting and interview and really ramps up when a new person comes on board.

Augmenting or sustaining a culture is difficult enough, but what if there is a need to change it? So often there is training and discussion and values documents, but Lueneburger offers an alternative view, addressing a case study that advises that the "trick is not to think yourself into a different way of acting . . . but to act yourself into a different way of thinking."[7] This is particularly compelling, particularly in terms of trying to bring change to an organization. Management theories often teach modeling your organizational values; this is the reverse—molding values through practice. This builds on the adage that actions speak louder than words; if individuals start to model the change they strive for, others will see it and do so as well.

Training and organizational development usually focus on skills acquisition or technical knowledge, but they are also an effective way to socialize new employees. Although less successful with long-term employees, training can also help orient them to changes in focus or climate. It is most effective if there is an effort to "chunk the work" or break up an project in manageable segments or tasks. A more incremental approach means that it is easier for people to adjust, easier to make modifications as the situation changes, and, overall, makes what seems a monumental task less overwhelming. In addition, for specific projects or initiatives, it allows discrete parts of a project to be assigned to a broad range of individuals who have diverse skills that each best fit a specific goal, thereby providing an inclusive environment and promoting buy-in.

Berry quotes a vice president of Service Master:

> Providing an environment which promotes the development of the whole person (from orientation and initial job skill training to personal development), enhances the dignity and worth of the individual service provider. In honoring the dignity of service through people development and people-focused management, we increase the motivation of the 'service partner' and thus can provide service that exceeds customer expectations.[8]

Interestingly, there are a number of excuses trotted out by organizations to abrogate the responsibility. One is that in a down economy, people are lucky to have a job (so it shifts the focus back to Maslow's lower-order needs). Another is that the next generation of workers won't stay in the job for very long before they go on to something better (so there is no need for loyalty of investment from either side), defaulting to a transactional relationship wherein individuals are disposable.

Play to people's strengths. Berry asserts that "People naturally gravitate to those roles for which they feel most competent—and avoid those for which they feel ill-equipped."[9] This also contributes to resistance to change and to lack of innovation. If an individual has no interest in a job or task, she is unlikely to put forth a lot of effort—which naturally impacts performance. This tendency is described in Bandura's theory of reciprocal determinism, which discusses the relationship between personal factors, behavior, and environment.

Equity is not about treating people the same; it is about fairness. "Every employee needs something different from a superior in order to perform up to his or her potential."[10] In terms of service provision, it may be that a subject-specialist librarian works with a specific department but focuses on instruction because she has both talent and commitment there, while a different specialist may focus on collection development or scholarly communication. Admittedly, this presents gaps in the services for different subjects, but these can be addressed if there is a more team-based structure that allows opportunity for collaboration and individual growth—and also provides a model that has support and built-in redundancy in the event that it is needed.

PERFORMANCE EVALUATION

A collective groan is often heard in an organization when it is time for performance evaluations, not merely because it is often a laborious process but also because even employees with positive performance are usually given feedback about improvement, so criticism is expected (and feared). This is generally when the process is pro forma, focused on ranking individuals for purposes of merit raises as opposed to developing their potential and remediating concerns.

Evaluations are not just uncomfortable for the employee being evaluated but also for the manager doing the evaluation. Ideally, there should be ongoing and honest conversations about the employee's performance and progress on individual goals. It seems that this hardly ever happens. It does require the difficult conversation, face-to-face, with specific examples so the employee knows what the problem is and how to address it.

Another point of frustration with evaluation processes, for personnel and also programmatically, is that the metrics are often meaningless in terms of the big picture: "measuring what you have accomplished is often impossible, given the absence of relevant yardsticks."[11] It is easy, in any profession, to measure activity—classes taught, books cataloged, patron visits—but that really is a measurement of activity and not impact. But even that measure of activity only fair in a superficial way—an engineering librarian may have few consults as compared to the English librarian who had a great number. They are comparable, right?

Wrong, and it is this perspective that can bring up concerns about procedural justice. It is necessary to measure the right things—and individual activity should be aligned with organizational priorities. That way the impact on the big picture is always in sight. "Service leadership significantly impacts organizational performance,"[12] which is indicated by the following:

- "Higher return on assets.
- More consumer and commercial accounts opened during the year.
- Higher reported levels of customer satisfaction and service quality.
- Higher levels of organizational commitment (loyalty) in employees.
- Higher levels of *esprit de corp* (teamwork) in the retail unit."[13]

REWARDS AND COMPENSATION

Evaluation and rewards are inextricably intertwined, both in the formal process and in the potentially less formal decision-making. To see what is truly important to an organization, don't look at mission statements or strategic plans, just follow the money. Organizations invest their money in what they truly think it important, whether it is what they purport to value or not. Employees in organizations spend their time doing what they are rewarded for, particularly when they have line of sight to the payoff for their efforts. Reinforcement theory payoff, similar to motivation, varies depending on the individual and may not be monetary— the motivating factor may be something else. This is especially true in public service organizations. Individuals can probably go elsewhere and make more money, so there is some other factor that keeps them there.

That is not to say that money does not play a role. In the most basic sense, employees need to be paid a living wage—that sends a powerful signal that the organization cares that they are taken care of and is not trying to take advantage. In the sense of procedural justice, the way that rewards are distributed and the comparison of pay needs to be transparent. This is not to suggest that transcripts of negotiations be made available, merely that what is valued is known and that individuals that do relatively similar jobs are paid relatively the same. "When resources and rewards or punishments are distributed to employees, the leader plays a major role. The rules that are used and how they are applied say a great deal about whether the leader is concerned about justice and how he or she approaches issues of fairness."[14] Too many discrepancies can demotivate people. When someone brings up a concern about pay, administrators are often heard to say, "We're not here for the money; it is about helping people." This is no doubt true, but there is some irony when an administrator making over $100,000 annually says this to a library employee making $35,000 a year. So, yes, we're not in it for the money, but we do expect fairness.

SERVICE LEADERSHIP IN PRACTICE

Lammert, a seasoned librarian known for his strong project management background, is facing yet another library reorganization. However, unlike the countless number of reorganizations before, Lammert was not consulted about who he was going to be reporting too. Soon after the reorganization was announced, Lammert discovered that he would be reporting to Wayne, an associate dean with a reputation of burning out his staff and taking all the credit for his staff's hard work. Within a week Lammert is given a new assignment—to complete an impossible project in an impossible deadline. When Lammert approached Wayne to discuss his concern, Wayne quickly dismissed his concerns with a simple "don't worry, you are a magician and you always end up pulling rabbits out of your hat." Lammert laughed nervously, knowing that he would have to put in a lot of overtime and work every night for the next two weeks to complete this impossible project. Two weeks later Lammert was sitting in the conference room proudly waiting Wayne's announcement to the rest of the library that Lammert had completed the project. To his surprise, it was the dean who walked up to the podium to make an the announcement that he was pleased that Wayne was able to complete an impossible project and that as a reward Wayne was to win the Librarian of the Year Award. Not only was Lammert confused but he was shocked to see Wayne stand up and accept the award without giving any recognition to Lammert or acknowledgement of the work that he had done.

ACCOUNTABILITY AND TERMINATION

The dichotomy of evaluation can lead to another outcome: disciplinary action or termination. As uncomfortable as the evaluation process may be, it also should be done with respect and care—and not only because of federal, state, and institutional regulations. How individuals are treated in a performance-development process, disciplinary action, or termination is watched closely by other employees with more than prurient interest: they want to understand how to avoid similar action themselves. If the process is not transparent, then it may inspire fear or mistrust. This is not to say that the personnel details should be made public; they should be kept strictly confidential. But the process should be adhered to and understood. In short, employees want to know that they are in a safe work environment.

While holding individuals accountable is a requirement for procedural justice, there should also be procedures to hold the organization accountable. These should provide a regular process for feedback about managers and administrators and an established mediation and grievance process. Employers, like employees, are entitled to feedback about their performance. This presupposes that there are expectations or standards for managers as well as individual goals; if not, they are working in a vacuum.

LEADERSHIP DEVELOPMENT AND SUCCESSION PLANNING

In this tough economic time, pay raises are no longer the sole incentive for motivating an employee to do a good job, and in service organizations, they are usually not the prime motivation regardless. People drawn to service organizations tend to be motivated by more altruistic factors. Dwindling library budgets mean that pay raises are becoming smaller and are unable even to match the increasing cost of living. In fact, over the past decade, a number of libraries across the United States have faced salary and hiring freezes, forcing many library employees to take on more work responsibilities for less money and to be thankful that they just have a job. Consequently, pay raises, or a lack thereof, can actually be a demotivator if library staff feel that their hard work goes unnoticed by the library director who, through no fault of her own, constantly tells them that there is no money for salary increases this year. However, there are additional incentives that service leaders can turn to in order to motivate their staff.

Personal and situational leadership theories, such as the Great Man theory, claim that the leader "created what the masses could accomplish,"[15] that people's imaginations were captured by the unique qualities of the leaders and that this was what motivated society to move forward.[16] These theories postulated that people were motivated by the personal traits of the leader, not because of what the leader was doing to support and serve the people.

One of the first formative leadership experiences is dealing with an individual employee. The experience leaves a footprint, regardless of whether the leader is effective or whether the experience is positive.. If this experience is profound enough, it will determine, to a large degree, how the leader deals with others—in other words, what kind of leader she will be.

Succession planning is fundamentally about an organization's sustainability, having individuals in the pipeline to move the organization forward. In some organizations, there is a hand-picked heir apparent who has been molded in the image of those in positional authority. This form of sustainability tends to be perceived as favoritism. However, it is possible to develop talent across the board so that there are individuals with varying skills and expertise to meet whatever situations the organization may face. The benefit of this approach is that it is perceived more equitably and the organization's talent pool is larger.

The additional benefit of having a large talent pool is that the organization's proverbial eggs are in a diversity of baskets. This matters for purposes of sustaining service, not just leadership. What happens when the librarian who administers the electronic course reserve system is on vacation for a week and the system goes down? Does someone else know how to address it? The issue can occur with any position that requires a specialized knowledge, access, or skill—service just stops. Telling a library user that the individual who can solve their problem won't be back for a week does not provide good service nor reflect well on the organization. Diversifying skills and promoting cross-training are ways to address this potential issue.

Mentoring is also a great way to build talent, pass on institutional knowledge, and promote collaboration: Beck states that "I've always tried to do more teaching or coaching or serving versus leading."[17] Haass discusses the role of a mentor or leader, saying "make sure they receive their fair share of the credit . . . shield them from criticism . . . help them develop their skills and advance their careers."[18] These relationships promote a sense of empowerment as well. "Empowering servers to serve is a necessary condition for delivering great service."[19] Berry describes empowerment as a state of mind in which one "experiences feelings of (1) *control* over how the job shall be performed; (2) *awareness* of the context in which the work is performed and where it fits in the "big picture"; (3) *accountability* for personal work output; (4) *shared responsibility* for unit and organizational performance; and (5) *equity* in the distribution of rewards based on individual and collective performance."[20]

Implicit in succession planning is the sharing of power or empowerment of others. This may be not be prevalent in libraries that have traditionally had a command-and-control culture: "Poor change leaders ...do not willingly share their power with others. Great change leaders, in contrast, allow those around them to take ownership, rather than monopolizing the change."[21] Instead of holding their authority close, people must give it away to others in the organization for the benefit of that organization. Ford asserts this as follows: "Transforming leaders are those who are able to divest themselves of their power and invest it in their followers in such a way that others are empowered . . ."[22] So does Wilkes, who says, "servant leaders multiply their leadership by empowering others to lead."[23]

This investment in the individuals in the organization models the commitment to the organization. While an extreme example, Northouse discusses the alternative: "For Burns, leadership has to be grounded in the leader-follower relationship. It cannot be controlled by the leader, such as Hitler's influence in Germany. Hitler coerced people to meet his own agenda and followed goals that did not advance the goodness of mankind."[24]

REFLECTIONS ON FORMALIZING SERVICE LEADERSHIP: TOOLS FOR DEVELOPMENT

1. Think about the library's organizational priorities. Do your job expectations and annual goals align with them?
2. What is the process of promotion in the library? Are expectations formalized so that individuals know what it takes to get to the next level?
3. Are there development opportunities for those who seek to advance or grow? How are these opportunities offered, do individuals indicate interest or are they selected?
4. Does the service culture permeate the organization? In other words, are internal patrons and colleagues treated as well as patrons?

NOTES

1. Darcy Jacobsen, "Wednesday Wisdom: Ten Quotes from Smart CEOs," www .globoforce.com/gfblog/2012/ten-quotes-from-ceos.
2. Bernard M. Bass and Ronald E. Riggio, *Transformational Leadership,* 2nd ed. (Mahwah, NJ: Lawrence Erlbaum, 2006), 126.
3. Ibid., 126–127.
4. Stephen R. Covey, "Serving the One," *Executive Excellence* 11, no. 9 (1994): 4.
5. Jason Geller, "There Is a Reason Why Companies Have Invested in HR: Without an HR Department the Void Will Be Rilled by Inexperienced Managers," (letter) *Wall Street Journal,* April 21, 2014, www.wsj.com/news/articles/SB10001424052702303626 80457950746167971938 6?mod=_newsreel_4.
6. Bernard M. Bass and Ronald E. Riggio, *Transformational Leadership,* 2nd ed. (Mahwah, NJ: Lawrence Erlbaum, 2006); Richard N. Haass, *The Bureaucratic Entrepreneur: How to be Effective in Any Unruly Organization* (Washington, DC: Brookings Institution, 1999), xii
7. Christoph Lueneburger, *A Culture of Purpose: How to Choose the Right People and Make the Right People Choose You* (San Francisco, CA: Jossey-Bass, 2014), 14.
8. Leonard L. Berry, *On Great Service: A Framework for Action* (New York, NY: Free Press, 1995), 190.
9. Ibid., 187.
10. Richard N. Haass, *The Bureaucratic Entrepreneur: How to be Effective in Any Unruly Organization* (Washington, DC: Brookings Institution, 1999), 105.
11. Ibid., 19.
12. Richard S. Lytle, "10 Elements of Service Excellence," *Texas Banking* 93, no. 6 (2004): 23.

13. Ibid.
14. Peter G. Northouse, *Leadership: Theory and Practice,* 6th ed. (Thousand Oaks, CA: Sage Publications, 2013), 389.
15. Bernard M. Bass, *Bass & Stogdill's Handbook of Leadership: Theory, Research, and Managerial Applications,* 3rd ed. (New York, NY: The Free Press, 1990), 37.
16. Thomas Carlyle, "On Heroes and Hero Worship (1841)," (Boston: Adams, 1897).
17. Curtis D. Beck, "Antecedents of Servant Leadership: A Mixed Methods Study," (dissertation, University of Nebraska), 76.
18. Richard N. Haass, *The Bureaucratic Entrepreneur: How to be Effective in Any Unruly Organization* (Washington, DC: Brookings Institution, 1999), 113.
19. Leonard L. Berry, *On Great Service: A Framework for Action* (New York, NY: Free Press, 1995), 208.
20. Ibid.
21. Christoph Lueneburger, *A Culture of Purpose: How to Choose the Right People and Make the Right People Choose You* (San Francisco, CA: Jossey-Bass, 2014), 23.
22. Leighton Ford, *Transforming Leadership: Jesus' Way of Creating Vision, Shaping Values & Empowering Change* (Downers Grove, IL: InterVarsity Press, 1991), 15.
23. C. Gene Wilkes, *Jesus on Leadership: Becoming a Servant Leader* (Nashville, TN: Lifeway Press, 1996), 25
24. Peter G. Northouse, *Leadership: Theory and Practice,* 6th ed. (Thousand Oaks, CA: Sage Publications, 2013), 393.

CHAPTER 10

SERVICE LEADERSHIP
IN LIBRARIES

Poor service has no redeeming virtue, nor does mediocre service
for that matter. Service excellence is more profitable, more fun,
and more conducive to a better future.
—*Leonard Berry*[1]

The quote above is from *On Great Service: A Framework for Action,* Leonard Berry's well-known book that explains how important it is for service organizations, such as libraries, to improve their service quality so that they can deliver what they promise and more. Librarians know that every service encounter consists of an interaction between the library and its users. This encounter, however, is no longer the traditional face-to-face interaction. Today library users are experiencing their libraries more and more through technology. In fact, ARL statistics show the dwindling face-to-face contact between librarians and their users. The increased use of electronic interfaces and material has empowered library patrons to find the information they need anywhere and at any time, not just when the library is open, and without the help of a librarian. Services and systems, such as the electronic interlibrary loan or even self-checkout of library material, that were traditionally behind the scenes and required face-to-face interaction with a librarian, are now available from the library's web page. When these behind-the-scenes library services, or any service, falls short and does not perform its promised functions, that service is not meeting the users' expectations. The user, unhappy with his experience with the service, may turn his back on the service and possibly the library. A user might even let others know about the bad service they received from the library. That is why the adage "You only have one time to create a good first impression" rings true. The interaction between the library and its patrons is critical to the library's success. User satisfaction is so important to any service industry. Rust, Moorman, and Dickson believe that corporations that focus on their customer's satisfaction and on the quality of service are generally more successful than companies that focus on cutting costs.[2] The reason for this is that higher satisfaction will increase patron loyalty to the company, helping to insulate a company's current market share from competitors, reduce operation costs, and reduce failure costs and thus the cost of attracting new customers, which will help build a firm's reputation. While Dickinson et al. address a corporate model, user satisfaction is perhaps even more critical for a public organization. While profit-driven organizations have a concrete metric of success, public organizations, libraries included, are selling an intangible service, one that is a public good and, as such, is hard to quantify. This means that the only meaningful metric is patron satisfaction. Librarians have the value of libraries diminished in the eyes of faculty members across academic institutions in both Canada and the United States. In a survey of 555 faculty members from 350 higher education institutions in these two countries, 82.13 percent indicated that they did not think that their library should be spending more on additional librarians.[3] This may indicate a disparity in expectation between librarians and those they serve—that fundamentally the library definition of service is not as relevant to our patrons. Many argue that service relates to encounters between the library and its patrons. Others equate service to the library profession itself, through activities performed in the library associations and committees. Some believe that it is service to each other—our colleagues and employees. However, service leaders would argue that service is all of these things and more. Service is not a transaction but a philosophy and a work ethic; it is a value that is modeled in all situations, regardless of the hierarchy or the power, regardless of the work environment.

Could the loss of value in academic institutions mentioned above indicate that libraries no longer know who they are serving and what they want? The key question that service leadership asks themselves is "Whom do libraries serve?" Despite the fact that this question is critical to the success of a service organization, it is often overlooked or dismissed with an arrogant and very short-sighted answer, such as "we know who our users are" or "we serve anyone who uses the library." An academic librarian might say that the library serves the students and teaching faculty of their institution. However, what if the library is funded by the taxpayers of a particular state? Does the library serve the person who lives three towns over who is trying to connect to the library's databases from their home computer but finds she can't because she is not affiliated to the library? Are we saying that she is not our user? How does she feel when she can't get the information she needs? Do these users believe that we don't serve them, even though they are paying for the library with their tax dollars? Why would they continue to support the library economically when the library is not supporting them?

EMPLOYEE AS THE PATRON

What about the library employees? Are they considered library users as they perform the day-to-day library functions? It would be short-sighted to say that library employees are not library users.

SERVICE LEADERSHIP IN PRACTICE

Samantha, an experienced electronic resource librarian, began negotiating a five-year licensing contract with a well-known journal publisher. After a hard negotiation Samantha was given 30 days to work out the contract logistics with her library administration. Pleased with the results and excited about her accomplishment, Samantha sent an e-mail requesting an appointment to discuss the contract agreements with her library business office. After three days without a response to her request, Samantha repeated her e-mail request and let the business office know that she had 30 days to finalize the agreement. Despite her urgent e-mail, once again her request for an e-mail response went unanswered. This silence continued, and after four e-mail attempts and multiple phone messages, Samantha turned to her supervisor for assistance. Even her supervisor was unsuccessful at organizing a meeting. Samantha was now distraught because she only had six days left to have the contract signed. Samantha was forced to speak to the dean about the lack of response and poor patron support from her colleagues in the business office. When asked about the lack of response by the dean, the business office said they were too busy with their patrons to help out Samantha. Surprised by the response, the dean was quick to reply that library employees in other units are the business office's patrons.

In the vignette above it is easy to see that it is not only important to identify which services you perform but also who your users are. Now take this a step further. Imagine how Samantha feels about the business office. Do you think that she believes that the business office is service oriented? Probably not! When asked to support the business office, do you think Samantha will volunteer to help? Will her opinion of the business office forever be jaded? Probably! Think about the effect of the poor treatment on Samantha; will this trickle down to the service Samantha offers to library patrons? Unfortunately, it may. Covey believes that there is a correlation between the ways leaders treat their employees and how these employees treat not only others in their organization but also their customers.[4] If employees are treated badly by their library colleagues, they will begin resenting how little they are valued and how badly they are being treated. Soon they will begin to model this bad treatment behavior to others, inside and outside of their organization. However, service leaders recognize that quality service, regardless of whether it is for an internal or external user, should be modeled by all employees to show that the patron is valued and respected by the service organization. Employees who are highly valued and well-trained by their organizations provide a higher level of service to their customers and patrons. A service leader's inclination is to serve first by focusing on the needs of the individual and to "treat all people with radical equality, engaging with others as equal partners in the organization."[5] Service leaders must continually assess how well each unit in the library is servicing each other unit. Where there is a breakdown in service support, the leader must address the issue. Grönfeldt and Strother support this by suggest the following actions for strengthening internal and external customer service orientation:

- "Employees should never complain within earshot of customers. It gives them the impression your company is not well run, shaking their confidence in you.
- Employees should never complain to customers about employees in other departments. Who wants to patronize a company whose people do not get along with each other?
- Employees at every level should strive to build bridges between departments. This can be done through cross-training and joint picnics, as well as day-to-day niceties.
- Use postmortems after joint projects so everyone can learn from the experience. Fences can be mended and new understandings gleaned when everyone reviews what went right or wrong. Not doing so can result in lingering animosities that will exacerbate future collaborations.
- Consider letting your employees become Customer of the Day to experience firsthand what your customers experience when doing business with you.
- Remember that service recovery applies to all customers—both internal and external."[6]

The key to building this relationship between units is for each employee to see the other employee not only as a team member but also as a customer who is playing a critical role in the organization's service supply chain.

PATRON PERCEPTION OF THE SERVICE CULTURE

It is a well-known fact that what people perceive to be the truth is their reality. When they witness bad service or experience bad service firsthand, they generally perceive the incident as something negative and it influences their opinion of future interactions. According to Weingand, "Among the library's customers, emotion is generally felt as a variation of anger or frustration."[7] Weingand believes that these twelve common interactions between the library and its customers that can produce these frustrations:

1. Customer is unable to locate materials or information.
2. Telephone is not answered promptly when customer calls.
3. Length of time until a reserved material is available seems too long.
4. Library staff is not friendly or helpful.
5. Library staff appears to be busy or unapproachable.
6. Parking is not available nearby.
7. Line at check-out is too long.
8. Librarian is not available to assist in locating material or information.
9. Customers are notified at inopportune times that requested items have arrived.
10. Library staff interpret policies literally and display a lack of flexibility.
11. Library hours are not convenient.
12. Customer must wait at the service desk while staff answers telephone.[8]

The above list, however, can be extended to include the following:

13. Customer is unable to maneuver through the library website.
14. Chat service technology does not work correctly and drops customers.
15. Library is too noisy.
16. Electronic material indicates availability but when tested is not available.
17. Electronic book and database layouts are not standardized making, it difficult to navigate between one technology and another.

No matter whether the user is an internal or external library patron, his perception becomes his reality and he has little or no desire to use or support the service again. The customer might even encourage others—friends, family members, or colleagues—not to use the service. Think about it, when was the last time you heard positive feedback about a library? Now think about the last time you heard something negative about a library. Library patrons are more likely to voice their anger, disappointment, expectations, and frustration with a library, as well as the perceived lack of respect, than they are to praise its good service. According to Peter Hernon, this is because "satisfaction is an emotional reaction—the degree of contentment or discontentment—with a specific transaction or service encounter. Satisfaction may or may not be directly related to the performance of the library on a specific occasion. A customer can receive an answer to a query but be unsatisfied because of an upsetting or angry encounter. Conversely, although the query might remain unanswered, another customer might feel satisfied because the encounter was pleasant and the helper interested and polite."[9] Service leaders know that satisfaction with a service does not necessarily equate to quality of the service. Hernon stresses that service quality "is a global judgment relating to the superiority of a service as viewed in the context of specific statements that the library is willing to act on if customers find them of great value. The inference is that this satisfaction levels from a number of transactions or encounters that an individual experiences with a particular organization fuse to form an *impression* of service quality for that person. The *collective* experiences of many persons create an organization's reputation for service quality."[10]

Disneyland, for example, has a reputation for being the happiest place on earth. One can say that this reputation is born out of the fact that the company recognizes the need to deliver high-quality customer service while making sure that their customers not only attain what they wanted in their Disneyland vacation but also create happy memories, which create a desire to return. Service leaders know that in order to give their patrons quality service they need to ensure that the patron receives what they came to the library for and also has a good experience while in using the library services.

PATRON'S PERCEPTION
OF EMPLOYEE'S INTERACTION

Interaction between patrons and employees is not the only concern that service leaders need to be attuned to. They also need to ensure that employees' interaction with each other models the values of the library so that patrons identify quality patron service with the organization. This is especially true in today's poor economic environment because it is commonplace to have student workers and support staff assigned to perform job duties that historically where handled by librarians. Gone are the days when it was solely the librarian who sat at the reference desk answering reference questions. In fact gone are the reference desks and reference collections in a large number of libraries in favor of a one service-desk model. Today the percentage of student workers and support staff working at public desks is extremely high, particularly during the nights, weekends, and holidays when most academic libraries experience the highest usage. A library patron rarely recognizes that it is not a librarian to whom they are speaking, and all the patron cares about is getting what he needs. Because of this staffing model shift, it is extremely important for service leaders to be aware of what happens at the desk at all times, not only between the library patron and the library employee but also between library employees.

Since patron service affects the organizational image, service leaders understand that delivering quality service is too important to be left to chance, and therefore, a plan must be created. In fact, delivering quality patron service is often the lifeblood of a library and therefore must be considered and constructed, when

SERVICE LEADERSHIP IN PRACTICE

Shannon, a freshman at a large academic institution, enters the library for the first time. Unsure of where to go and who to ask for help, she looks around shyly in hope of finding someone to help her. Within seconds she identifies a public service desk but is hesitant to approach it because she sees two employees deep in what looks like an argument. As she slowly approaches the desk, she begins to hear part of their conversation and is taken aback by the tone used by one librarian as he speaks to his colleague. Surprised that the two employees would be having such a heated conversation in public, Shannon shook her head in disappointment at their lack of professionalism. At no time did they make eye contact with her and at no time did they recognize her presence. As she stood there waiting for one of the two librarians to make eye contact with her, she began to feel uncomfortable while the librarians continued their verbal battle. Disappointed and frustrated, Shannon turned away from the desk thinking she wasn't going to get help from this desk, so she better figure it out on her own.

possible, before library patrons encounter the library. In the sidebar above, it is easy to see the initial impact of this type of poor patron service. The patron not only did not receive any service from the library but she left disappointed and frustrated at the employees' lack of professionalism. When students, who may pay a library user fee on top of the public taxes that fund public academic libraries, experience poor patron service like Shannon did, they may feel like they are paying an employee that isn't working.

PATRONS' PERCEPTION OF LIBRARY SERVICE

From the example above, it is easy to see that that library patrons form attitudes about the library, its employees, and library services based on what they see and experience. It is important to note that not all services are delivered face-to-face. More and more library patrons come to the library virtually through the library website, chat, or phone reference and through electronic access of books and journals. Despite how the patron gains access to material, Zeithaml et al. identified five core criteria by which customers evaluate service quality. They are defined as follows:

1. Tangibles: physical facilities, equipment, and appearance of personnel;
2. Reliability: ability to perform the promised service dependably and accurately;
3. Responsiveness: willingness to help customers and provide prompt service;
4. Assurance: knowledge and courtesy of employees and their ability to inspire trust and confidence; and
5. Empathy: caring, individualized attention the organization provides its customers.[11]

As more and more patrons demand that their library come to them, demands for electronic access will increase. Patron expectations of libraries will vary, however, according to what patrons want and how urgently they want it. Think about a time when you needed to help a patron find an article for a paper she was writing, but the patron waited until the night before the paper was due to get help from the library. It is easy to see that importance and urgency of the information need can influence how satisfied a patron is with a library service.

Leaders can help mitigate these negative service encounters by:

- setting and continually communicating the organization's service vision, goals, and values to the library employees to foster organizational commitment;
- modeling the organization's commitment to its service vision, goals, and values;
- committing to empowerment efforts so that employees can solve immediate problems;
- ensuring that each employee is sufficiently trained to perform his job duties;
- encouraging employees to try and not punishing them for failing;
- rewarding employees for service excellence;
- listening to the concerns of employees and acting on suggestions when necessary;
- supporting employees by recognizing that the patron is not always right;
- holding themselves and employees accountable for their actions; and
- admitting when they are wrong.

SERVICE QUALITY

In order to manage service quality, you need to be able to measure what service quality is and how it is applied to your library. Oakleaf stresses that "libraries have long argued that they are integral to the teaching and learning mission of higher education. Now, libraries must prove that they contribute to the production of quality graduates."[12] To do this libraries need to develop appropriate metrics to assess service. This will allow the library to measure service activities, making them visible and tangible, and to quantify the library's service achievements and failures for its stakeholders.

However, trying to get librarians to agree on the metrics can be difficult and may be like trying to herd cats. Despite this disagreement, regardless of what metrics are chosen to benchmark the library services, the metrics need to identify performance strengths so that quality service performance is recognized and rewarded and at the same time identify performance weaknesses that need to be addressed. It is also critical that these balanced metrics help monitor progress toward the library's mission, vision, and goals. According to Grönfeldt and Strother, "it is crucial that the organization make sure the metrics fit the company's culture, values, and its way of doing things. For example, an organization known for teamwork and a collective sales approach might decide to apply measures of individual performance and even go as far as to link payments to those metrics only if it wants to change its ways. Such measures could destroy rather than reinforce its traditional way of operating. Furthermore, the metrics need to address results and direct behaviors so they can be used to develop or enhance individual or group performance."[13] Oakleaf stresses that "in the past, libraries have relied heavily on input, output, and process measures as key indicators of excellence. These measures are no longer considered adequate for assessing the impact of libraries' services on college students. In a climate of outcomes-based measurement, university stakeholders are less interested in traditional measurements: the count of the volumes on library shelves, the number of students checking out books, or the speed with which reference questions are answered. Rather, they want libraries to determine what students know and are able to do as a result of their interaction with the library and its staff."[14] Service leaders must develop a way of identifying metrics so that they do not deviate from the library's culture, values, and its way of doing things because deviation can create conflict, not only between the services and values but also between the employees who are performing the services. Grönfeldt and Strother believe that a strategic map, such as the one developed by Kaplan and Norton in the 1990s, is an effective way for a service leader to visualize how her organization can connect its goals and strategies and communicate clear cause-and-effect relationships for their employees.[15] Once the goals and strategies are identified, a tool to gather the information, such as SERVQUAL, can be used to measure the service quality in the library and what library patrons value.

Building on the *Millennium Librarian*'s Standards of Behaviors, the following can be used to help librarians develop good patron service etiquette for their library.[16]

1. Greet patrons with a smile and a pleasant face as they enter the library. If you're frowning, you are going to give the wrong impression.
2. Treat all patrons the same—provide equitable service and attention.
3. Expect your staff to treat patrons with courtesy and respect, to be polite, and to be willing to help. Never let them act rude or bossy.
4. Expect your staff to be treated with courtesy and respect.
5. Create welcoming physical and virtual spaces.
6. Encourage your staff to answer telephone calls and/or chat reference in a courteous and polite manner. Note that whether you are dealing with patrons in person or on the phone, the way you begin a conversation or interaction will affect how the patron treats you; first impressions are hard to change.
7. Generate rapport. When a client approaches you, your greeting should be short and to the point. But sometimes it is more appropriate to spend a bit of time in conversation before getting down to business. Spend a minute or two asking questions or talking about subjects other than the reason patron is there. The purpose is to establish a relationship with the individual or to recognize that a relationship already exists.
8. Encourage your staff to answer questions in a prompt and timely manner—don't let the telephone ring more than twice.
9. Be firm if you need to be and remind patrons of policies, rules, and procedures.
10. Don't break library policy or procedures. If you do, how will you enforce those rules? Remember that it is hard to enforce a policy if employees are not abiding by it.
11. Encourage your staff to excuse themselves and get a supervisor if they are having difficulty with a patron or group of patron.
12. Encourage your staff to build a user-friendly website that is easy for patrons to navigate.
13. Encourage your staff to ensure that electronic access to items is working and that broken links are fixed.

ORGANIZATIONAL CULTURE

As discussed in previous chapters, each library develops its own organizational culture that is founded on the norms of the library employees and becomes manifested in their behavior and actions. The term *organizational culture* means "the collective assumptions, value systems, and norms that groups develop to cope with problems of external adaption and internal integrations."[17] Although the underlying values of libraries are the same, their organizational cultures vary considerably. One library may have a traditional organizational structure in which each employee must get the permission of their supervisor to sneeze. Other more forward-focused libraries have a less traditional organizational structure in which the library director encourages her employees to take risks and be empowered to make decisions. According to Moran et al., a library's "organizational culture comes from three main sources: 1) the beliefs, assumptions, and values of the organization's founder; 2) the learning experiences of group members as the organization evolves; and 3) fresh beliefs, values, and assumptions brought in by new members and leaders."[18] Consequently, it is easy to see how a library's organizational culture can affect staff morale and how this can affect the way staff members interact with library patrons. According to Weingand, "Librarians with even the best service orientation will find it problematic to provide a high level of service if the operating environment does not encourage and empower the staff to provide this level of service. Conversely, library staff with less enthusiasm for customer service to begin with may be energized when management encourages and rewards a positive service attitude."[19]

SERVICE LEADERSHIP IN PRACTICE

John, a 13-year veteran of access services, moves to a new departmental library on a large academic campus. John has heard his new supervisor say that she encourages her staff to embrace change and try new things. John is excited to work with a manager who promotes risk-taking performance and empowers them to make decisions. He couldn't wait to jump into his new position. Two days after John begins his new position, he decides to make an exception for a library patron. He let the patron know that it was an exception and that the library would not be able to do this again. When Lillia, his supervisor, discovers what he did, she is upset and tells John that he stepped outside of his realm of responsibility and that he should have come to her to make sure the exception was acceptable. John was shocked. All he did was allow the patron to check out a low-use book for one extra day. He couldn't understand why Lillia was making such a big deal about his decision. When he asked her why he was wrong, all Lillia could say was, "because I said so."

In the sidebar above, it is easy to see what happens if library administration says one thing but models another. John witnessed firsthand how Lillia encouraged empowerment in her employees, but when he acts on that encouragement, she punishes him for showing initiative. When this happens it creates an organizational culture of distrust and frustration. In order to avoid this type of negative culture and sustain quality service, organizational culture service leaders must model the values they promote.

Figure 10.1 offers a representation of the interdependence of these values in the progression toward the ideal of service leadership. The ladder indicates the reliance of each upward stage on the preceding stage: if one step is removed, such as *self-awareness*, the individual regresses back to the previous stage, regardless of how far he had previously progressed. Note that the ladder's rails are *encouragement/accountability* and *service commitment* respectively. These elements are critical to the development of the service leadership ethic: the individual must have internalized that service commitment and the environment in which they operate must support encouragement and accountability. Should the environment change, whether due to new management or changing values, the rail of encouragement and accountability is destabilized and the ladder of service leadership falls apart.

REFLECTIONS ON SERVICE LEADERSHIP IN LIBRARIES: TOOLS FOR DEVELOPMENT

1. When discussing an issue with your team members, try modeling the library's mission values and goals to see if the team also begins modeling the same behavior.

2. Think about the official channels of communication: what is the message that is communicated? Now consider the unofficial channels of communication: is the message consistent or is the grapevine very active and critical? Does it paint a different and potentially more representative picture of actions and decisions in the library? What does this say about the organization?

3. The next time you enter the library, stop and sit down. Watch how your team members interact with one another. Think about what you know about the individuals. Does the interaction seem normal to you? Does one person have a stronger personality than the other? Now pretend you are a library patron and know nothing about these employees. Does the interaction between employees seem normal? Does the communication seem cordial? Is one team member helping out the other team member or are the interactions seem more like a conflict?

Figure 10.1   Service Leadership

4. Consider cross-training as a way to help facilitate communication between different units, opening up dialog to incorporate a different perspective towards service. Have a cataloger sit at a public service desk and vice-versa so that each can get a perspective on the other's idea of public service and how each's regular duties impact the other unit.

NOTES

1. Leonard L. Berry, *On Great Service: A Framework for Action* (New York, NY: Free Press, 1995), 3.
2. Roland T. Rust, Christine Moorman, and Peter R. Dickson, "Getting Return on Quality: Revenue Expansion, Cost Reduction, or Both?," *Journal of Marketing* 66, no. 4 (2002): 7–24.

 3. Primary Research Group, *The Survey of Higher Education Faculty: Level of Faculty Satisfaction with the Academic Library* (New York, N.Y.: Primary Research Group, 2009), 89.
 4. Stephen R. Covey, "Serving the One: The Key to the Many Is the One," *Executive Excellence* 11, no. 9(1994): 5–6.
 5. Sen Sendjaya, James C. Sarros, and Joseph C. Santora, "Defining and Measuring Servant Leadership Behaviour in Organizations," *Journal of Management Studies* 45, no. 2 (March 2008): 407.
 6. Svafa Grönfeldt and Judith Strother, *Service Leadership: The Quest for Competitive Advantage* (Thousand Oaks, CA: Sage Publications, 2006), 167–168.
 7. Darlene E. Weingand, *Customer Service Excellence: A Concise Guide for Librarians* (Chicago, IL: American Library Association, 1997), 73.
 8. Ibid., 73.
 9. Peter Hernon and Allen Altman, *Assessing Service Quality: Satisfying the Expectations of Library Customers,* 2nd ed. (Chicago, IL: American Library Association, 2010), 5.
10. Ibid.
11. Valarie A. Zeithaml, A. Parasuraman, and Leonard L. Berry, *Delivering Quality Service: Balancing Customer Perceptions and Expectations* (New York: The Free Press, 1990), 26.
12. Megan Oakleaf, "Dangers and Opportunities: A Conceptual Map of Information Literacy Assessment Approaches," *portal: Libraries and the Academy* 8, no. 3 (2008): 233.
13. Svafa Grönfeldt and Judith Strother, *Service Leadership: The Quest for Competitive Advantage* (Thousand Oaks, CA: Sage Publications, 2006), 177.
14. Megan Oakleaf, "Dangers and Opportunities: A Conceptual Map of Information Literacy Assessment Approaches," *portal: Libraries and the Academy,* 8, no. 3 (2008): 233–234.
15. Svafa Grönfeldt and Judith Strother, *Service Leadership: The Quest for Competitive Advantage* (Thousand Oaks, CA: Sage Publications, 2006), 177–178.
16. The Millennium Librarian, May 22, 2010, http://millenniumlibrarian.blogspot .com/2010/05/customer-service-in-libraries.html.
17. Barbara B. Moran, Robert D. Stueart, and Claudia J. Morner, *Library and Information Center Management,* 8th ed. (Santa Barbara, CA: Libraries Unlimited, 2013), 132.
18. Ibid., 132–333.
19. Darlene E. Weingand, *Customer Service Excellence: A Concise Guide for Librarians.* (Chicago, IL: American Library Association, 1997), 5.

BIBLIOGRAPHY

Agel, Jeromen, and Walter D. Glanze. *Pearls of Wisdom: A Harvest of Quotations from All Ages*. New York: Harper Row, 1987.

Aguilar, Francis Joseph. *Scanning the Business Environment*. New York: Macmillan, 1967.

Alzheimer's Association. www.alz.org.

American Library Association. www.ala.org/advocacy/advleg/advocacyuniversity/ frontline_advocacy/frontline_public/goingdeeper/swot.

Anzalone, Filippa Marullo. "Servant Leadership: A New Model for Law Library Leaders." *Law Library Journal* 99, no. 4 (2007): 793–812.

Autry, James A. *The Servant Leader: How to Build a Creative Team, Develop Great Moral, and Improve Bottom-Line Performance*. New York: Prima, 2001.

Bakker, Arnold, and Wilmar Schaufeli. "Positive Organizational Behavior: Engaged Employees in Flourishing Organizations." *Journal of Organizational Behavior* 29, no. 2 (2008): 147–154.

Bass, Bernard M., and Bruce J. Avolio. "Transformational Leadership and Organizational Culture." *Public Administration Quarterly* 17, no. 1 (1993): 112–121.

Bass, Bernard M., *Bass & Stogdill's Handbook of Leadership: Theory, Research, and Managerial Applications*, 3rd ed. New York: The Free Press, 1990.

Bass, Bernard M., and Ronald E. Riggio. *Transformational Leadership*, 2nd ed. Mahwah, NJ: Lawrence Erlbaum, 2006.

Beck, Curtis D., University of Nebraska at Lincoln. "Antecedents of Servant Leadership: A Mixed Methods Study," Dissertation (2010).

Bell, Arthur H., and Dayle M. Smith. *Management Communication*. New York: Wiley, 1999.

Bennis, Warren. *On Becoming a Leader*. New York: Perseus Books, 2009.

Bennis, Warren, and Burt Nanus. *Leaders: The Strategies for Taking Charge*. New York: Harper & Row, 1985.

Berry, Leonard L. *On Great Service: A Framework for Action*. New York: Free Press, 1995.

Berry, Leonard L., Valarie A. Zeithaml, and A. Parasuraman. "Five Imperatives for Improving Service Quality." *MIT Sloan Management Review* 31, no. 4 (1990): 29–38.

Bozeman, Barry. *All Organizations are Public: Comparing Public and Private Organizations*. Washington, DC: Jossey-Bass, 1987.

Bradford, David V., and Allan R. Cohen, "The Postheroic Leader." *Training and Development Journal* 38, no. 1 (1984): 40–49.

Branson, Robert K., et al. Interservice Procedures for Instructional Systems Development. Executive Summary and Model. Florida State Univ. Tallahassee Center for EducationalTechnology, 1975, www.dtic.mil/dtic/tr/fulltext/u2/a019486.pdf.

Buchanan, Leigh. "In Praise of Selflessness: Why the Best Leaders Are Servants." *Inc. Magazine,* May 2007.

Burley-Allen, Madelyn. *Listening: The Forgotten Skill: A Self-Teaching* Guide, 2nd ed. New York: John Wiley, 1995.

Burns, James MacGregor. *Leadership.* New York: Harper & Row, 1978.

Carlyle, Thomas. *On Heroes and Hero Worship.* Boston: Adams, 1897.

Caruso, David R., and Peter Salovey. *The Emotionally Intelligent Manager: How to Develop and Use the Four Key Emotional Skills of Leadership.* San Francisco, CA: Jossey-Bass, 2004.

Charan, Ram. "Why CEOs Fail." *Fortune* 139, no. 12 (1999): 68–75.

Conger, Jay A., and Beth Benjamin. *Building Leaders: How Successful Companies Develop the Next Generation.* New York: Wiley and Sons, 1999.

Conger, Jay A., and Rabindra N. Kanungo. "Toward a Behavioral Theory of Charismatic Leadership in Organizational Settings" *The Academy of Management Review* 12, no. 4 (1987): 637–647.

Conger, Jay A., Rabindra N. Kanungo, Sanjay T. Menon, and Purnima Mathur. "Measuring Charisma: Dimensionality and Validity of the Conger-Kanungo Scale of Charismatic Leadership." *Canadian Journal of Administrative Sciences* 14, no. 3 (2009): 290–301.

Covey, Steven R. *Principle Centered Leadership.* New York, NY: Simon & Schuster, 1992.

Covey, Stephen R. "Serving the One: The Key to the Many is the One," *Executive Excellence* 11, no. 9 (1994): 5–6.

Covey, Stephen R. *The 7 Habits of Highly Effective People: Powerful Lessons in Personal Change.* New York: Free Press, 2004.

Daniel, Teresa A. *Stop Bullying at Work: Strategies and Tools for HR and Legal Professionals.* Alexandria, Va.: Society for Human Resource Management, 2009.

Davis, Tim R., and Fred Luthans. "Leadership Reexamined: A Behavioral Approach," *Academy of Management Review* 4, no. 2 (1979): 237–248.

DeGraaf, Don., Colin Tilley, and Larry Neal, "Servant-Leadership Characteristics in Organizational Life." In *Practicing Servant Leadership: Succeeding through Trust, Bravery, and Forgiveness,* edited by L. C. Spears and M. L. Lawrence, 133–165. San Francisco: Jossey-Bass, 2004.

Devonish, Dwayne. "Workplace Bullying, Employee Performance and Behaviors: The Mediating Role of Psychological Well-Being." *Employee Relations* 35, no. 6 (2013): 630–647.

Dewey, Barbara I. "Public Services Librarians in the Academic Community: The Imperative for Leadership." In *Leadership and Academic Librarians*, edited by Terrence F. Mech and Gerard B. McCabe, 85–97. Westport, CT: Greenwood Press, 1998

Disney, Walt. Brainy Quote.com. www.brainyquote.com/quotes/quotes/w/ waltdisney132637.html.

Doncevic, John. "Servant-Leadership as a Model for Library Administration." *Catholic Library World* 73, no. 3 (2003): 171–178.

Drucker, Peter R. *Management Tasks, Responsibilities, Practices*. Oxford: Butterworth Hienemann, 1974.

Dupree, Max. *Leadership Is an Art*. East Lansing, MI.: Michigan State University Press, 1987.

Dyer, Frank Lewis., and Thomas Commerford Martin. *Edison, His Life and Inventions*. Hyperion Works, 2014. Downloaded from Project Gutenberg.

Fairholm, Gilbert W. *Perspectives on Leadership: From the Science of Management to its Spiritual Heart*. Westport, CT: Quorum Books, 1998.

Farnsworth, Kent Allen. *Leadership as Service: A New Model for Higher Education in a New Century*. Westport, CO: Greenwood, 2007.

Ferrell, O., M. Hartline, G. Lucas, D. Luck. *Marketing Strategy*. Orlando, FL: Dryden Press, 1998.

Forbes. October 2, 2012. www.forbes.com/sites/ashoka/2012/10/02/12-great -quotes-from-gandhi-on-his-birthday

Ford, Leighton. *Transforming Leadership: Jesus' Way of Creating Vision, Shaping Values & Empowering Change*. Downers Grove, IL: InterVarsity Press, 1991.

Frick, Don M. *Robert K. Greenleaf: A Life of Servant Leadership*. San Francisco: Berrett-Koehler, 2004.

Fromm, Erich. "Selfishness and Self-Love." *Psychiatry, Journal for the Study of Interpersonal Process* 2 (1939): 507–523.

Garner, Eric, *The Art of Leadership* 46. http://stritapiret.or.id/wp-content/ uploads/2013/03/the-art-of-leadership.pdf.

George, Bill. *Authentic Leadership: Rediscovering the Secrets to Creating Lasting Value*. San Francisco: Jossey-Bass, 2003.

George Bush Award for Excellence in Public Service (College Station, TX). As Delivered by Secretary of Defense Robert M. Gates, College Station, TX, Friday, October 26, 2007. www.defense.gov/Speeches/Speech.aspx?SpeechID=1190.

Gobillot, Emmanuel. *Follow the Leader: The One Thing Great Leaders Have that Great Followers Want*. Philadelphia: Kogan Page Publishers, 2013.

Goleman, Daniel, Richard Boyatzis, and Annie McKee. *Primal Leadership: Realizing the Power of Emotional Intelligence*. Boston: Harvard Business School Press, 2002.

Gore, Al, World Class Courtesy: A Best Practices Report, A Report of the National Performance Review. http://govinfo.library.unt.edu/npr/library/papers/ benchmrk/courtesy/intro.html 15.

Greenleaf, Robert. *On Being a Servant Leader,* ed. Don M. Frick and Larry C. Spears. San Francisco: Jossey-Bass, 1990.

Greenleaf, Robert K. *The Power of Servant-Leadership,* ed. Larry C. Spears. San Francisco: Berrett-Koehler, 1998.

Greenleaf, Robert K. *Servant Leadership: A Journey into the Nature of Legitimate Power & Greatness.* Mahwah, NJ: Paulist, 1977.

Greenleaf, Robert K. *Servant Leadership: A Journey into the Nature of Legitimate Power & Greatness.* New York: Paulist Press, 2002.

Greenleaf, Robert K. *The Servant Leader Within: A Transformative Path.* Mahwah, NJ: Robert K. Greenleaf Center, 2003.

Grönfeldt, Svafa, and Judith Strother. *Service Leadership: The Quest for Competitive Advantage.* Thousand Oaks, CA: Sage Publications, 2006.

Haass, Richard N. *The Bureaucratic Entrepreneur: How to be Effective in Any Unruly Organization.* Washington, DC: Brookings Institution, 1999.

Hennessy, Beth A., and Terisa M. Amabile. "Conditions of Creativity." In *The Nature of Creativity: Contemporary Psychological Perspectives,* edited by Robert J. Sternberg. New York: Cambridge University Press, 1988: 11–38.

Hernon, Peter, and Allen Altman. *Assessing Service Quality: Satisfying the Expectations of Library Customers,* 2nd ed. Chicago: American Library Association, 2010.

Herzberg, Fredrick I. *Work and the Nature of Man.* Cleveland, OH: World Publishing, 1966.

Hogan, Robert, Gordon J. Curphy, and Joyce Hogan. "What We Know About Leadership: Effectiveness and Personality." *American Psychologist* 49, no. 6 (1994): 493–504.

Hughes, Richard, Robert Ginnett, and Gordon Curphy. *Leadership: Enhancing the Lessons of Experience,* 3rd ed. Boston: Irwin McGraw Hill, 1999.

Hunter, James C. *The Servant: A Simple Story About the True Essence of Leadership.* New York: Random House, 2012.

Jacobsen, Darcy. "Wednesday Wisdom: Ten Quotes from Smart CEOs." www .globoforce.com/gfblog/2012/ten-quotes-from-ceos.

James, William. "Great Men, Great Thoughts, and Their Environment." *Atlantic Monthly* 46 (1880): 441–459.

Jehn, Karen A., Gregory B. Northcraft, and Margaret A. Neale. "Why Differences Make a Difference: A Field Study of Diversity, Conflict and Performance in Workgroups." *Administrative Science Quarterly* 44, no. 4 (1999): 741–763.

Kanungo, Rabindra, and Manuel Mendonca. *Ethical Dimensions of Leadership.* Thousand, Oaks, CA: Sage Publications, 1996.

Kontakos, Anne-Marie. "Employee Engagement and Fairness in the Workplace." *Center for Advanced Human Resources Studies* (2007): 18–32.

Kornacki, Susan A., and David R. Caruso. "A Theory-Based, Practical Approach to Emotional Intelligence Training: Ten Ways to Increase Emotional Skills." In

Applying Emotional Intelligence: A Practitioner's Guide, edited by Joseph Ciarrochi and John D. Mayer, 53–88. New York: Psychology Press, 2007.

Kouzes, James M., and Barry Z. Posner. *The Leadership Challenge,* 3rd ed. San Francisco: Jossey-Bass, 2002.

Kovel-Jarboe, Patricia. "Quality Improvement: A Strategy for Planned Organizational Change." *Library Trends* 44, no. 3 (1996): 605–630.

Kreitz, Patricia A. "Leadership and Emotional Intelligence: A Study of University Library Directors and Their Senior Management Teams." *College & Research Libraries* 70, no. 6 (2009): 531–554.

Lakos, Amos, and Shelley Phipps. "Creating a Culture of Assessment: A Catalyst for Organizational Change." *portal: Libraries and the Academy* 4, no. 3 (2004): 345–361.

Larson, Colleen L., and Khaula Murtadha. "Leadership for Social Justice." *Yearbook of the National Society for the Study of Education* 101, no. 1 (2002): 134–161.

Leban, Bill and Romuald Stone, *Managing Organizational Change,* 2nd ed. Hoboken, NJ: John Wiley, 2008.

Lencioni, Patrick M. *Getting Naked: A Business Fable about Shedding the Three Fears That Sabotage Client Loyalty.* San Francisco: John Wiley & Sons, 2009.

Lueneburger, Christoph. *A Culture of Purpose: How to Choose the Right People and Make the Right People Choose You.* San Francisco, CA: Jossey-Bass, 2014.

Tytle, Richard S. "10 Elements of Service Excellence." *Texas Banking* 93, no. 6 (2004): 22–27.

Martin, Jason. "The Art of Librarianship: Thoughts on Leadership Skills for Next Generation of Academic Library Leaders." *College & Research Libraries News* 70, no. 11 (2009): 652–654.

Maslow, Abraham Harold. "A Theory of Human Motivation." *Psychological Review* 50, no. 4 (1943): 370–396.

Matarazzo, James M. "Recruitment. The Way Ahead." In *Recruiting, Educating, and Training Cataloging Librarians. Solving the Problems,* edited by Sheila S. Intner and Janet Swan Hill. New York: Greenwood Press, 1989.

Mayer, John, Peter Salovey, David R. Caruso, and Gill Sitarenios. "Emotional Intelligence as a Standard Intelligence." *Emotion* 1, no. 3 (2001): 232–242.

McCarthy, Dan. "What is Leadership? 30 Definitions." http://management.about .com/od/leadership/fl/What-is-Leadership-30-Definitions.htm.

McFarlin, Dean B., and Paul D. Sweeney. "Distributive and Procedural Justice as Predictors of Satisfaction with Personal and Organizational Outcomes." *Academy of Management Journal* 35, no. 3 (1992): 626–637.

McCraven, Admiral William H. "Adm. McRaven Urges Graduates to Find the Courage to Change the World." University of Texas at Austin, commencement address. www.utexas.edu/news/2014/05/16/admiral-mcraven-commencement -speech.

Megginson, Leon C. "Lessons from Europe for American Business." *Southwestern Social Science Quarterly* 44, no. 1 (1963): 3–13.

The Millennium Librarian. "Customer Service in the Libraries." *The Millennium Librarian* (May 22, 2010): millenniumlibrarian.blogspot.com.

Moran, Barbara B., Robert D. Stueart, and Claudia J. Morner. *Library and Information Center Management*, 8th ed. Santa Barbara, CA: Libraries Unlimited, 2013.

Morgenstern, Jim, and Rebecca Jones. "Library Strategic Planning: Voyage of Starship Enterprise or Spruce Goose?" *Feliciter* 58, no. 5 (2012): 12–14.

National Performance Review (US), and Albert Gore. *World-Class Courtesy: A Best Practices Report: A Report of the National Performance Review.* (The Review, 1997).

Ng, Kok-Yee, and Christine S.-K. Koh. "Motivation to Serve: Understanding the Heart of the Servant-Leader and Servant Leadership Behaviors." In *Servant Leadership: Developments in Theory*, edited by Dirk van Dierendonck and Kathleen Patterson. New York: Macmillan, 2010: 90–104.

Northouse, Peter G. *Introduction to Leadership: Concepts and Practice.* Thousand Oaks, CA: Sage Publications, 2009.

Northouse, Peter G. *Leadership: Theory and Practice.* Thousand Oaks, CA: Sage Publications, 2010.

Northouse, Peter G. *Leadership: Theory and Practice*, 6th ed. Thousand Oaks, CA: Sage Publications, 2013.

Nye, Joseph S. *Soft Power: The Means to Success in World Politics.* New York: Public Affairs, 2004.

Nye, Joseph S. *The Powers to Lead.* New York: Oxford University Press, 2008.

Oakleaf, Megan. "Dangers and Opportunities: A Conceptual Map of Information Literacy Assessment Approaches." *portal: Libraries and the Academy* 8, no. 3 (2008): 233–253.

Olson, Nancy J. "Refreshing Your Philosophy of Servant Leadership as a Christian Librarian." *Christian Librarian* 53, no. 2 (2010): 48–55.

Parolini, Jeanine, Kathleen Patterson, and Bruce Winston. "Distinguishing Between Transformational and Servant Leadership." *Leadership and Organization Development Journal* 30, no. 3 (2009): 274–291.

Patterson, Kathleen Ann. "Servant Leadership: A Theoretical Model. Regent University." Dissertation (2003).

Pearson, Christine M., and Judith A. Clair. "Reframing Crisis Management." *The Academy of Management Review* 23, no. 1 (1998): 59–76.

Pinchot, Gifford. *Intrapreneuring.* New York: Harper & Row, 1985.

Primary Research Group. *The Survey of Higher Education Faculty: Level of Faculty Satisfaction with the Academic Library.* New York: Primary Research Group, 2009.

Quinn, James Brian, Jordan J. Baruch, and Penny Cushman Paquette. "Technology in Service." *Scientific American* 257, no.6 (1987): 50–58.

Rennaker, Mark A. *Listening and Persuasion: Examining the Communicative Patterns of Servant Leadership* (dissertation). Virginia Beach, VA: Regent University, 2008.

Renz, David O., and associates, *The Jossey-Bass Handbook of Nonprofit Leadership and Management*, 3rd ed. San Francisco: Wiley, 2010.

Riggs, Donald E. "The Crisis and Opportunities in Library Leadership." *Journal of Library Leadership* 32, no. 3/4 (2011): 5–17.

Riggs, Donald E. "The Crisis and Opportunities in Library Leadership." In *Library and Information Science Professions*, edited by Mark D. Winston. Binghamton, NY: Haworth Press, 2001.

Riggs, Donald E. "Visionary Leadership." In *Leadership and Academic Libraries*, edited by Terrence F. Mech and Gerard B. McCabe. Westport CT: Greenwood Press, 1998.

Rogers, Everett M. *Diffusion of Innovations*, 5th ed.. New York: Free Press, 2003.

Russell, Robert. "The Role of Values in Servant Leadership." *Journal Leadership and Organization Development* 22, no. 2 (2000): 76–83.

Russell, Robert F. and A. Gregory Stone. "A Review of Servant Leadership Attributes: Developing a Practice Model." *Leadership and Organization Development Journal* 23 no. 3 (2002): 145–157.

Rust, Roland T., Christine Moorman, and Peter R. Dickson. "Getting Return on Quality: Revenue Expansion, Cost Reduction, or Both?" *Journal of Marketing* 66, no. 4 (2002): 7–24.

Saks, Alan M. "Antecedents and Consequences of Employee Engagement." *Journal of Managerial Psychology* 21, no. 7 (2006): 600–619.

Salovey, Peter, and John D. Mayer. "Emotional Intelligence." *Imagination, Cognition and Personality* 9, no. 3 (1989–90): 185–211.

Schreiber, Becky, and John Shannon. "Developing Library Leaders for the 21st Century." In *Leadership in the Library and Information Science Professions*, edited by Mark Winston, 35–49. Binghamton, NY: Haworth, 2001.

Seeger, Matthew W. *Ethics and Organizational Communication*. Cresskill, NJ: Hampton Press, 1997.

Sendjaya, Sen, and Brian Cooper. "Servant Leadership Behaviour Scale: A Hierarchical Model and Test of Construct Validity." *European Journal of Work and Organizational Psychology* 20, no. 3 (2011): 416–436.

Sendjaya, Sen, James C. Sarros, and Joseph C. Santora. "Defining and Measuring Servant Leadership Behavior in Organizations." *Journal of Management Studies* 45, no. 1 (2008): 402–424.

Senge, Peter. "Leading Learning Organizations: The Bold, The Powerful, and the Invisible." In *The Leader of the Future*. San Francisco: Jossey-Bass 1996: 41–58.

Senge, Peter. *The Fifth Discipline: The Art & Practice of the Learning Organization*. New York: Doubleday, 1990.

Senge, Peter. "The Leader's New Work: Building Learning Organizations." *Sloan Management Review* 32, no. 1 (1990): 7–23.

Sipe, James W., and Don M. Frick. *Seven Pillars of Servant Leadership: Practicing the Wisdom of Leading by Serving*. Mahwah, NJ: Paulist Press, 2009.

Skinner, B.F. *Science and Human Behavior*. New York: Free Press, 1953.

Spears, Larry C. "The Understanding and Practice of Servant-Leadership." In *Practicing Servant Leadership: Succeeding through Trust, Bravery, and Forgiveness,* edited by L. C. Spears and M. Lawrence, 9–24. San Francisco: Jossey-Bass, 2004.

Spears, Larry C. "Tracing the Past, Present, and Future of Servant-Leadership." In *Focus on Leadership: Servant-Leadership for the Twenty-First Century,* edited by Larry C. Spears and Michele Lawrence. New York: Greenleaf Center for Servant-Leadership, 2002.

Steil, Lyman K., Larry L. Barker, and Kittie W. Watson. *Effective Listening: Key to Your Success*. Reading, MA: Addison-Wesley, 1983.

Stoffle, Carla, Robert Renaud, and Jerilyn R. Veldof. "Choosing our Futures." *College & Research Libraries* 57, no. 3 (1996): 213–225.

Strother, Judith B., and Svafa Grönfeldt. "Service Leadership: The Challenge of Developing a New Paradigm." *2005 IEEE International Professional Communications Conference Proceedings* (2005): 65–71.

Sweet Manager Blog, "10 Quotes on Strategy," http://sweetmanager.blogspot .com/2013/05/10-quotes-about-strategy.html.

Taylor, Robert. "Question-Negotiation and Information Seeking in Libraries." *College & Research Libraries* 29 (1968): 178–194.

Trevino, Linda K. *Ethical Leadership: Creating an Ethical Culture*. 2005. www.scu .edu/ethics/practicing/focusareas/business/conference/presentations/Trevino .ppt.

Trompenaars, Fons and Ed Voerman. *Servant-Leadership Across Cultures*. New York: McGraw Hill, 2010.

Tzu, Lao, and Tao Te Ching. "Listening to Ourselves." In *Listening to Conflict: Finding Constructive Solutions to Workplace Disputes,* edited by Erik J. Van Slyke, 33–64. New York: American Management Association, 1999.

vanDuinkerken, Wyoma, Wendi Arant Kaspar, and Jeanne Harrell. *Guide to Ethics in Acquisitions*. New York: Scarecrow Press, Inc., 2014.

Van Wart, Montgomery. *Dynamics of Leadership in Public Service: Theory and Practice,* 2nd ed. Armonk, NY: M.E. Sharpe, 2011.

Vera, Dusya, and Mary Crossan. "Strategic Leadership and Organizational Learning." *The Academy of Management Review* 29, no. 2 (2004): 222–240.

Vondey, Michelle. "The Relationships Among Servant Leadership, Organizational Citizenship Behavior, Person-Organization Fit, and Organizational Identification." *International Journal of Leadership Studies* 6, no. 1 (2010): 3–27.

Geller, Jason. "There Is a Reason Why Companies Have Invested in HR: Without an HR department the void will be filled by inexperienced managers." [letter] *Wall Street Journal.* (April 21, 2014). www.wsj.com/news/articles/SB100014240 527023036268045795074616797193386?mod=_newsreel_4

Walters, Suzanne. *Customer Service: A How-To-Do-It Manual for Libraries.* New York: Neal-Schuman, 1994.

Weingand, Darlene E. *Customer Service Excellence: A Concise Guide for Librarians.* Chicago: American Library Association, 1997.

Wilder, Stanley J. *The Age Demographics of Academic Librarians: A Profession Apart.* New York: Routledge, 2000.

Wren, J. Thomas. *The Leader's Companion: Insights on Leadership Through the Ages.* New York: The Free Press, 1995.

Wilkes, C. Gene. *Jesus on Leadership: Becoming a Servant Leader.* Nashville, TN: Lifeway Press, 1996.

Yang, Song. "A Contextual Analysis of Organizational Commitment." *Sociological Focus* 36, no. 1 (2003).

Yukl, Gary. *Leadership in Organizations,* 6th ed. Upper Saddle River, NJ: Prentice Hall, 2006.

Zeithaml, Valarie A., A. Parasuraman, and Leonard L. Berry. *Delivering Quality Service: Balancing Customer Perceptions and Expectations.* New York: The Free Press, 1990.

INDEX

....

D

Daniel, Teresa, 68
Darwin, Charles, 78
decision-making and values, 36–37
DeGraaf, Don, 45
development and mentoring, 115–118
development tools. See tools for development
Devonish, Dwayne, 68
Dewey, Barbara I., 75
Dickson, Peter R., 139–140
direct service models, 79
Disney, Walt, 73
distributive justice, 65
diversity, 112–113
Drucker, Peter R., 92
Dupree, Max, 121

E

Edison, Thomas, 76
Einstein, Albert, 4
emotional blueprint, 62
emotional intelligence, 10, 61–63
empathetic listening, 46–47, 50
employee as customer, 140–142
empowerment, 63–65, 135
encouragement and accountability
    emotional intelligence, 61–63
    empowerment, 63–65
    influence, 57–58
    overview, xiii, 57
    personal accountability as a library leader,
        58–61
    social and procedural justice, 65–69
    termination and accountability, 133–134
    tools for development, 69–70
entrepreneurs, librarians thinking like, 80
environmental scan, 99
ethical egoism, 37
ethical leadership, 11, 37–38
evolving service. See innovation and evolving
        service
exemplary leadership, five practices of, 9

F

failure, behaviors leading to, 58
fair treatment of employees, 66
favoritism, 67, 128–129, 134
feedback, 69, 83
Filek, Robert, 90
filtering out superfluous or repetitive information
        to get at the facts, 52
Follow the Leader (Gobillot), 3
Ford, Leighton, 135

formalizing service leadership in libraries
    accountability and termination, 133–134
    leadership development and succession
        planning, 134–136
    learning and personnel development,
        129–131
    overview, xvi–xvii, 125–127
    performance evaluation, 131–132
    recruitment and selection, 127–129
    rewards and compensation, 132
    tools for development, 136
Franklin, Benjamin, 94
Freedom to Read Statement (ALA), 38

G

Galton, Francis, 4
Gates, Robert M., 17
George, Bill, 10
goals, 93–94
Gobillot, Emmanuel, 3
Goleman, D., 10
Great Man theory, 4, 5, 134
Greenleaf, Robert, 13–14, 29, 31, 49, 53, 111
Grönfeldt, Svafa, 15, 16, 22, 74, 78, 80, 142,
        147

H

Haass, Richard N., 77, 84, 112, 130, 135
Heller, Joseph, 96
Hernon, Peter, 143
Hersey, Paul, 4
Herzberg, Frederick, 118
hiring process, 127–129
Hogan, Robert, 50
honesty and integrity, 33–34
House, Robert, 9
Hughes, Richard, 75
human resources (HR), 126
Humphrey, Albert, 97
Hunter, James C., 58

I

influence, 57–58
informational diversity, 113
innovation and evolving service
    challenging the process, 84–85
    change, 78–79
    change management, 80–83
    creativity, 74–76, 78
    innovation defined, 75
    motivating factors for, 74
    overview, xiii–xiv, 73–74
    risk taking, 84–85